*Praise for*
# TRIBESPOTTING

"It's hard to keep track of the sheer number of subcultures in the world today—and yet reading *Tribespotting*, it appears as if Harmon Leon's infiltrated them all. This book was eye-opening to say the least, taking me to places I'd never heard of (including some I maybe wish I still hadn't)."

–David Litt, author of *NY Times* bestseller *Thanks, Obama*

"No one infiltrates better than Harmon Leon. For a three month period in the summer of 2010, I thought he was my George Foreman grill. But yes, I've been a fan for a long time: from *Republican Like Me* to *Meet the Deplorables* to *Tribespotting*. He's the installation artist I would want to be if I didn't spend all my time yelling. (Tough to infiltrate while yelling.)"

–Lee Camp, head writer and host of *Redacted Tonight*

"My fave? Perhaps that anarcho-situationist rave-up SantaCon? Or the Furries? Or … or … Harmon Leon takes us inside some fairly troubled American Dreams."

–Anthony Haden-Guest, author of *The Last Party*

"*Tribespotting* lifts the lid on the strangest and most surreal corners of the country. If you thought the U.S. was bizarre before, you haven't seen nothing yet."

–Harriet Alexander, *The Daily Telegraph*

*Praise for*

## HARMON LEON

"Anyone can mock their ideological enemies, but in *Meet the Deplorables*, Harmon Leon does something revolutionary here—he actually gets to know them. A natural, endlessly engaging storyteller, Leon's forays into Trump America are fascinating, funny, and incisive. Gonzo journalism at its finest."
 –Davy Rothbart, creator of *Found Magazine*, author of *My Heart Is an Idiot*

"If you've had the courage to peek out of your asshole and take a gander at our devolving America, you won't be shocked the evils and inequities that Harmon Leon takes to task in *Meet the Deplorables*. But you'll be amazed how he can make us laugh as we slowly swirl down the muddy toilet."
 –Doug Stanhope, author of *This Is Not Fame: A "From What I Re-Memoir"*

"*Meet the Deplorables* is a rollicking ride through Trumpland; Leon takes you on a tour of the stranger side of the States. By turns laugh-out-loud funny and poignant, it's a vital guide to understanding what is happening in America today."      –Harriet Alexander, US Correspondent for *The Daily Telegraph*

"I got more of a sense of Trump's voters from [*Meet the Deplorables*] than from a lot of other reporting."      –Nancy Updike, producer of *This American Life*

"[Harmon Leon is] funny as hell."                                         –Howard Stern

"You cannot but be amazed by the sheer guts of Harmon Leon."
 –Carol Kolb, former editor-in-chief of *The Onion*

"[Harmon Leon is] one funny motherfucker!"            –Jimmy Kimmel

"Dangerous ... Endlessly entertaining ... Read [*The American Dream*]; it's fantastic."                                                            –Carson Daly

*Also by*
## HARMON LEON

*Meet the Deplorables:*
*Infiltrating Trump America*
(with Ted Rall)

*The American Dream:*
*Walking in the Shoes of Carnies, Arms Dealers, Immigrant Dreamers,*
*Pot Farmers, and Christian Believers*

*The Infiltrator:*
*My Undercover Exploits in Right-Wing America*

*Republican Like Me:*
*Infiltrating Red-State, White-Ass, and Blue-Suit America*

*The Harmon Chronicles*

*National Lampoon's Road Trip USA*

*The Brothers Rjukerooka*

# TRIBESPOTTING
## UNDERCOVER CULT(URE) STORIES

# TRIBESPOTTING
## UNDERCOVER CULT(URE) STORIES

## HARMON LEON
### CARTOONS BY KEITH KNIGHT

**39 WEST PRESS**
Kansas City, MO
www.39WestPress.com

# 39 WEST PRESS

Text Copyright © 2019 by Harmon Leon
*(th)ink* and *The K Chronicles* Cartoons Copyright © 2019 by Keith Knight

All rights reserved.

No part of this book may be reproduced, scanned, or distributed in any printed or electronic form, including information storage and retrieval systems, without permission. Please do not participate in or encourage piracy of copyrighted materials in violation of the author's rights.

Please purchase only authorized editions.

First Edition: November 2019

ISBN: 978-1-946358-20-2

Library of Congress Control Number: 2019930910

10 9 8 7 6 5 4 3 2 1

*Book Design, Edits: j.d.tulloch*

39WP-28-P

To My Tribe: *My Friends and Family*

# CONTENTS

*Preface*      *xvii*

## A GATHERING OF THE TRIBES

| | |
|---|---:|
| Machine Gun Shooters | 5 |
| Furries | 12 |
| Viral Video Fans | 20 |
| Drunk Santas | 28 |

## FOR CHRIST'S SAKE

| | |
|---|---:|
| Hookers for Jesus | 39 |
| Jump for Jesus | 46 |
| Body-slammin' for Jesus | 53 |

## LIVE FOR FREE OR DIE HARD

| | |
|---|---:|
| Freegans | 63 |
| Squatters | 68 |

## SILLY, SILLY WHITE FOLKS

Fans of Jerry Springer   81
Tanning Addicts   88
White Supremacists   93

## COMEDY TO THE RESCUE

Presidential Joke Writers   105
Cuban Comics   112
Christian Comics   117
Fans of "The Juice"   127

## THEY JUST WANNA BE LOVED

Trophy Wife Hunters   141
Pickup Artists   152

## THEIR TRIBES ARE CULTS

The Raëlians   163
Staring Cult   170

*Afterword*   181

*Acknowledgments*   183
*Image Credits*   185
*About the Author*   187

*The individual has always had to struggle to keep from being overwhelmed by the tribe. If you try it, you will be lonely often, and sometimes frightened. But no price is too high to pay for the privilege of owning yourself.*

–**Friedrich Nietzsche**

*Spice Girls is about unifying the world—every age, every gender, everyone. It's woman power; it's an essence, a tribe.*

–**Geri Halliwell**
**(Ginger Spice)**

# LET'S DO SOME TRIBESPOTTING

Harmon Leon with OJ Simpson on the set of *Juiced*.

# PREFACE

IN MY PREVIOUS BOOK, *Meet the Deplorables: Infiltrating Trump America*, I ventured deep into Red State territory to explore the political divisiveness in the United States by examining the motivations behind those who helped propel Donald J. Trump to the White House. Two years later, our country is even more divided. We exist as two separate tribes, fighting to provoke, condemn, and defeat the other.

While *tribalism* may be the latest catchword used by politicians and pundits to describe the "us" versus "them" mentality currently playing out in American culture, the concept is not new. Since the beginning of civilization, humans have organized themselves into tribes. According to Andrew Sullivan, this type of communal cohesion was essential to survival, and in many ways, it's the default human experience, which comes to us more naturally than any other way of life. Thus, it's quite normal that we, as humans, seek out and join with others who share similar interests and goals. We all want to be among like-minded people. We all want to be accepted. And we all want to belong. Tribes, therefore, provide a sense of belonging and community while allowing us to unite with our fellow enthusiasts.

However, in this current age of tribalism, where conflicting ideologies define individuality and provide no room for comprise, empathy and discussion are non-existent, demonization and vilification of the other run rampant, and mob mentality prevails. Despite the fact that we all are Americans and should share common societal goals, it is now nearly impossible to converse with fellow citizens who embrace views that oppose our own.

As a member of a tribe, it's easy to paint those who have opposing ideas with broad strokes and view them as one-dimensional enemies that applaud eating babies, taking away our guns, or allowing caravans of invading gang members across our borders so that they can rampage our city streets and date our loved ones.

In *Tribespotting: Undercover Cult(ure) Stories*, I dive directly into the eye of the tribal storm, changing my look and attitude as I go undercover in an exploration of tribal behavior and its many manifestations throughout modern culture. Using the same inimitable style that I have honed while infiltrating extremist groups, I introduce readers to a series of vastly different tribes, including machine gun lovers and white supremacists, freegans and squatters, pickup artists and trophy bride seekers, and furries and viral video stars. Some of these tribes engage in harmless, hobby-loving fellowship while others revolve around the adulation of charismatic celebrities. Some of these tribes strive to uplift the individual via religious enlightenment and a few are actually full-blown cults. But at the root of all these different tribes lies the same psychological need—the desire to be around like-minded people.

With that in mind, let's do some tribespotting.

# A GATHERING OF THE TRIBES

## TRIBES
Machine Gun Shooters
Furries
Viral Video Fans
Drunk Santas

## TRIBAL LEADERS
Jungle Walk Bob
Mad Scientist, Inventor of the Dragon Vagina
Connor Franta / Joey Graceffa / Rosanna Pansino
John Law

## WHERE TO SPOT TRIBE MEMBERS
Knob Creek Gun Range
Further Confusion
Stream Con
SantaCon

## TRIBAL TRAITS
Heavily Armed
Dressed in Animal Costumes
Carrying iPhones and Selfie Sticks
Clad in Santa Suits Covered in Vomit

# MACHINE GUN SHOOTERS

**B**IG-BELLIED MEN CLAD IN plaid flannel shirts and entire families outfitted in camouflage fatigues exited a parking lot full of pickup trucks and paraded towards the entrance gate. "Welcome machine gun shooters!" proclaimed a sign tacked to the gate. For some reason, I had decided to spend a fun-filled weekend with five thousand assault weapon enthusiasts at the bi-annual Machine Gun Shoot & Military Gun Show at the Knob Creek Gun Range, which is, of course, located in Bullitt County, Kentucky.

"Are there going to be helicopters this year?" inquired a man sporting a mullet haircut and wearing a *No Trigger Locks* T-shirt. As I shuffled past him and through the gate, the sound of gunfire, like giant crashing waves, filled the air. Immediately, a hardened Christian woman handed me a pamphlet for Camp America: *Where God's Truth and Patriotism Go Hand in Hand.*

"It teaches people about the Constitution," she tried to explain as a man who claimed to fear Social Security numbers interrupted with paranoid ramblings about the conspiracy literature he was peddling.

This event was possibly the whitest one I had ever attended. Most people, many of whom looked as if they were harboring terrible secrets, wore holstered guns as fashion accessories. A large portion of the men easily could have passed as the guys in ZZ Top while others painted their faces in order to seem less conspicuous. Had I known costumes were a part of the ritual, I would have dressed as a pirate.

For many attendees, however, the Machine Gun Shoot was a family affair. If anything, the little kid factor was endearing: most of the boys looked like Bobby from the television show *King of the Hill*.

"Mustache Bob, your gun's ready at the firing range!" blasted the loudspeaker as heartily fed Americans sat on bleachers and waited for the shooting spree to begin.

"What I want to try is a jetpack!" a man exclaimed with childlike enthusiasm while gleefully watching a helmeted performer in a silver astronaut suit blast a burnt-out car with apocalyptic orange fire spraying from the end of a flamethrower.

"Girl Scout bake sale!" shouted a group of little girls selling crumbled cakes at a table inside a tent showroom, which was also filled with row after row of assault weapons. If I ever had aspirations of starting my own country in the woods, this place was where I'd begin.

"How much for this gun?" I asked, putting the dealer's crusty head in the sight of his very own AK-47.

"Five thousand bucks," barked the old, Southern geezer.

That was a little too much for my budget, so I moved on to something I could afford: his array of racist bumper stickers. As I sifted through the neatly arranged piles, he stared at me, transfixed with a glazed look of pure, engraved bigotry, wondering which maliciously subtle one I would choose: *The Original Boys In the Hood* (featuring a picture of three hooded Klansmen), a Confederate flag with *It's A White Thing! Christian America!*, or *Aids Cures Fags!*

Unable to find a bumper sticker that represented by beliefs, I wondered why he didn't have a bumper sticker that proclaimed: *We Hate Anyone Who Isn't Us!*

Looking for an out, a guy carrying a rifle passed by. His T-shirt, which caught my attention, announced to the world:

*CHRISTIAN*
*AMERICAN*
*PRO-GUY*
*HETEROSEXUAL*
*ANY QUESTIONS?*

I quickly pointed my camera at him.

"Don't take my picture!" he barked at me. "I don't want you taking my picture."

I retorted, "Hey, I'm not going to argue with a guy with a gun."

The Christian, American, pro-guy heterosexual grunted, "Whatever!"

I knew that was how it always starts: a few exchanges and then blam-blam-blam—argument over!

Speaking of gunfire, a large blast of exploding bullets suddenly snapped me back to reality. It was LOUD … really fucking loud! It was so loud that it made sweat run down my back. It was so loud that nearly everyone felt the need to scream at each other like complete fuck-wits. My point: it was LOUD!

As a result, tracking down the nearest provider of ear protection became my first priority, but not before almost bumping into a burly skinhead with a pit bull at his side.

With earplugs procured, I was off to the shooting range. Like a giant video game come to life, the shooting range was scattered with shot-up cars, large wooden spools, and, for some reason, ovens. The only thing missing was "bad men" dodging between obstacles, attempting to achieve a high score.

Large American flags flapped proudly over the shooting area. A spray-painted red line designated where the large, surging crowd should stand. On the other side of the line, numerous assault weapons discharged a rapid-fire spray of bullets as empty shells flew everywhere. Safety standards seemed an afterthought. One guy fired too soon, shooting a line of bullets just feet in front of him.

"Whatever's cookin' in there is done!" screamed a Grizzly Adams look-alike.

The orange-shirted security personnel, and myself, were the only people without guns. But that was about to change. I spotted three vendors renting a multitude of assault weapons and machine guns: everything from M16s to AK-47s. It was time to blow up some shit!

I waited in line behind a pimply-faced kid with braces who was wearing a *Skynyrd Kicks Ass* T-shirt.

"Come on! It's a once in a lifetime thing," he begged, trying to convince his friend to shoot with him.

"Which gun is the most fun?" I screamed over the gunfire at a guy with a long beard who was handing out loaded clips. He recommended the Fire Monster, a .308 caliber HK51.

"God damn!" announced a man who had just finished using the Fire Monster. "God damn!"

As the bearded guy reclaimed the weapon from the man, he declared, "I know what you'll be dreaming about!"

Next, a proud father pointed his son to the Fire Monster.

"It's his first time," boasted the father.

Like other "first times," the kid was nervous. Then, like an old pro, he fired away and was all smiles when finished.

"You won't forget that," shouted the bearded man.

"That's a little different than a video game," added his dad.

"I got to get me one of those!" said the delighted kid.

Finally, it was my turn to experience the thrills of the Fire Monster. I leaned hard into the weapon.

"Put the flipper on twenty, and you're ready to rock and roll!"

Blam! Holy shit! I felt like Chow Yun Fat in *Hard Boiled*. It was like having a flippin' tank on my shoulder. Dirt flew from the ground like exploding mini-landmines. The firepower thrust me backward, and the bearded man put his hand on my back to steady me. After shooting the Fire Monster, I felt downright giddy, which probably wasn't a good thing.

"God bless you," I said to the bearded man as I handed back the Fire Monster to him.

After the instant euphoria began to wane, I decided that it was time to try another weapon.

"You're back!" said the bearded man.

I was happy to be recognized as a repeat customer. That time I selected a 9mm Uzi with a thirty-shot clip. Compared to the Fire Monster, shooting the Uzi was like slicing through butter. There was very little kick as I sprayed the targets with a sea of bullets.

"Take that, bitch!" I screamed while blasting bullet-riddled cars and ovens.

The Uzi jammed. A guy in a white Panama hat came to the rescue and adjusted the weapon. Then, it was back to rapid-fire shooting. The whole thing was over in twenty seconds. I handed the Uzi back to the bearded guy, feeling like such a sportsman.

"I got to get one of these for school," I mumbled. "Fucking teachers."

Finally, it was time for the Jungle Walk, where participants ran through a muddy path in the woods while carrying a fully loaded assault weapon and trying to shoot eighteen different stationed targets, all while being timed with a stopwatch. This ridiculous event must have been organized by the same genius who invented "running through the house with scissors."

The Jungle Walk check-in was near a banner that displayed a drawing of a Vietnamese man and the handwritten words "Kill Charlie." I signed-up with Bob, an old guy wearing glasses, who sat next to a skull on a stick with the words "Yank You Die" written across the forehead. Was the Jungle Walk some sort of weird Vietnam War flashback for Bob?

"We came all the way from Austria for this," boasted a pair of bug-eyed Austrians who waited in line behind me.

"You know, I was impressed by the Austrian army when I was over there in '68," said the commando who was in charge of the Jungle Walk. The man, decked out in fully army fatigues, handed the Austrians a flyer that outlined the World War II battle reenactments.

"I read about this," admitted one of the excited Austrians.

"See, we don't have a problem with this in the States," the commando informed with pure American pride.

After a quick briefing in which everyone present strained to listen as a result of the steady blasts of gunfire, the commando provided one final bit of advice: "If you want to be John Wayne, that's up to you." Then, just as a gun went off in the woods behind us, he pointed an Uzi directly at my face and added, "Lean into it, across your body."

Momentarily, I saw my life pass before my eyes. SHIT!!! That scared the living fuck out of me!

"This is for you guys!" the commando screamed.

As I waited for three yobs from Cleveland to finish the course, I put my secondary clip in my back pocket and prepared to fire my fifty rounds. Bob stood behind me with a stopwatch.

"Ready ... Go!"

I took off running with my loaded Uzi, and Bob followed behind with his ticking stopwatch.

"Look through the sight," coached Bob.

Taking his advice, I fired at a metal plate attached to a tree before sprinting to the next station, where I blasted several coffee cans sitting atop some short poles.

"I'm hit," I proclaimed after a hot shell flew out of the Uzi and struck me in the neck. I was actually wounded by my own goddamn flying shrapnel! But, as a brave soldier, I was not going to let a measly shrapnel wound end my mission. I gathered myself and ran, with blood streaming down my neck, to the final station. It was just me, and Bob, alone in the woods.

At approximately seventeen hundred hours, the upper shooting range resembled downtown Baghdad. Cars were on fire, and pillars of black smoke filled the sky. Enough artillery had been fired to fend off several insurgent armies. It was pure insanity: the love of mass destruction, the love of America, and the thrill of violence all rolled in to one Kentucky afternoon. I felt as if I were Don Quixote screaming at the midday sun.

But I wasn't. My ears hurt, and I had a huge, bloody welt on my neck.

In the end, all I could do was treat myself to a snow cone. But it was not to be. The vendor scooped the ice from the bin with his bare, dirty hands and formed it into a snowball. Disgusted, I immediately threw the filthy snow cone into the trash and called it a day.

# FURRIES

**N**UMEROUS QUESTIONS CROSSED MY mind while looking at the simulated dragon vagina. From under a blue cloth, a mad scientist unveiled the Fem Dragon to the crowd. "This is the prototype," he stated in a thick, Scottish accent. Unfortunately, the Fem Dragon wasn't yet available for human use. During product testing, he explained, it was discovered that "we made the hole too small!"

At first, I was moderately impressed that someone was able to create the scaly sexual reproductive organs of a mythical, fire-breathing creature. Then, it suddenly dawned on me that I was looking directly at a man who willingly had "made sweet love" to a simulated dragon vagina. But since the man claimed to have lived a past life as a *dragonkin*, a powerful and intelligent dragon-like creature, dragon-related carnal relations, naturally, would have been second nature to him.

This sexy toy impresario was just one of the thousands of *furries* who had congregated at the Doubletree Hotel in San Jose for Further Confusion (or FurCon), the country's second largest gathering of furries, people who have an interest in anthropomorphic animals and/or creatures that possess human or superhuman capabilities.

Some furries suit up in elaborate animal costumes while others merely sport animal tails and ears.

Originally, furries were interested in only popular furry cartoon characters, known as "funny animals," such as Bugs Bunny or Tony the Tiger. A furry dark side soon evolved from its innocent beginnings. Members of this niche group, known as furverts (or yiffs), are sexually aroused by the animal/human hybrid experience and like to partake in sex while adorned in full furry regalia. Now, these deviant troublemakers, the seedy anthropomorphic black sheep of the furry family, come to FurCon alongside the wholesome furries who attend to learn things such as team mascot skills or how to draw rabbits.

Yiffs, according to traditionalists, have created a negative reputation for furries by spawning media interest only in the sexual aspect of their community. Hollywood, in particular, has helped facilitate the deviant furvert stereotype. For example, a *CSI* episode ("Fur and Loathing") followed a murder case linked to a furpile, a furry orgy (or yiffing). And on an episode of *Entourage*, Johnny Drama donned a pink bunny suit—with a hole cut out for easy access to his privates—so that he could bone a squirrel costumed furry who yelped woodland noises while in the throes of sex.

As a result of these media representations, many traditional furries feel as if they've been pushed to the back of the fantasy-role-playing bus. But I wanted to find out for myself. So, I threw together a bunch of random accessories (a pig mask, bear ears, and a furry vest) leftover from previous Halloween costumes and was off to infiltrate the world of furry fandom.

The lobby of the Doubletree looked like the furry equivalent of the canteen in *Star Wars*—or possibly a Timothy Leary acid trip. A sea of furries mingled as the hotel staff watched with bemused expressions. Some furries were dragged around on leashes. Two coyotes teasingly simulated oral sex, and a pair of wolves made out before playfully communicating via mime.

"Welcome to the village. You've been hugged, tagged, and sent back to the community," a wolf/human hybrid announced to a man in shorts, thus initiating him into the pack.

Even though the attendees were roughly ninety percent male, the convention was not entirely devoid of attractive women. Large IT-looking guys sporting animal tails flirted with the few female furries, which included a big-breasted cat with pink hair, a curvy wolf draped in a tight dress, and a belly-dancing, yellow-haired giraffe. The interaction between Dungeons & Dragons-types and a corset-clad horse resembled a creepy Halloween celebration.

"Thank goodness there are a lot of other freaks out there to join me!" exclaimed a furry named Chad. "I get all giddy dressing up as a giant, furry rat! We're all ridiculous. I choose to put my pride aside and simply party how I wish to."

The complete anonymity was fun. My pig mask provided me with the cover I needed to schmooze at leisure.

"Where's the dogs?" someone playfully jested at what appeared to be the cast of Cats scampering by. The German-speaking felines—to catcalls of "here kitty, kitty, kitty"—posed for snapping cameras.

"We outgrew the Doubletree years ago," shared a photographer. "I came here in '98, and you could fit all the costume characters into one hotel room."

In an attempt to change their fur-suit-bonking image, Further Confusion required that the Doubletree's lobby remain a PG-13 zone. Collars and leashes could be worn discreetly, but "anatomically correct" costumes had to be covered where it counted. Apparently, a few "anatomically correct" mishaps had occurred at past conventions. Furthermore, groping, tongue battles, nudity, and blatant displays of BDSM were not allowed in public and could result in the revocation of one's badge. But that threat didn't stop a wolf and a lion from manhandling each other and a group of men from grinding on a rodeo dog.

At the bar, a large humanoid, who called himself "Trendevar," nursed a beer. "There are usually lots of wolves and foxes, some cats," he said. "This year we have some horses and deer. I even saw a Minotaur!" Trendevar had adopted what sounded like a furry name, even though he wore human clothes.

"Why do you think people are so into anthropomorphic characters?" I asked him.

"For ages, anthropomorphic animals were there to teach us lessons about overcoming adversity and learning from our mistakes," Trendevar reasoned. "Like Aesop's fables, kids learn because they can relate to the animal kingdom."

I wondered to myself what kinds of lessons could be learned from a simulated dragon vagina and costumed furry sex with a Minotaur.

But, remember, not all furries came to FurCon to bang simulated dragon vaginas or Minotaurs while wearing their costumes. "I don't really go in for the fur-suit sex," said Zuki, who was attired as a large mythical beast with green eyes and fangs. "It's way too uncomfortable in one of those costumes to have much fun, and you'll only ruin an expensive piece of work!"

Fur suits can range from five hundred to eight thousand dollars, and it can take a skilled craftsman up to eighty hours to construct a complex fur head, some of which include movable animatronics. "The costumes with stripes are more expensive because they need to be hand-sewn," interjected Trendevar. "The more elaborate costumes have fans built in."

All attention turned to a dog in an intricate fur suit that was engineered to appear as if it were walking on all fours. Zoran XT followed the canine as it waddled toward an area with a large sign that read: "Please only fur suits and helpers. No photos or video."

"What goes on there?" I asked.

"This is the Headless Lounge," announced the gatekeeper. "This is where people come to chill out and take their heads off 'cause it gets hot!"

After adjusting my pig mask, I entered the secret lounge. Industrial-sized fans attempted to cool off the severely dehydrated-looking furries, whose heads hung from a nearby rack. Sewing machines and glue were on hand for fur-suit emergency repairs.

"That's certainly a big, red costume," commented a heavyset woman while brushing the yellow mane of a furry horse head. The headless Clifford did not reply.

Then, a group of busty female furry characters entered the lounge. A sexy, corset-wearing horse, with huuuge tightly bound breasts, removed her head, and it was ... a dude! A sexy coyote/fembot also removed her head, revealing ... another dude! More heads were removed; more dudes were revealed. It seemed as if I were trapped in some weird furry *Crying Game* full of an entire flock of cross-dressing men, complete with tails, corsets, big breasts, and fake J. Lo booties. Many issues were being explored there.

"After much engineering, I finally got the cleavage to work. It's a gel," said the corseted horse-man while pointing to his big boobs.

"That's sexy," replied the fembot coyote-dude. "I got this makeup in New Zealand."

The horse-man then invited other men to come over for a feel. One guy even thrust his head between the gel breasts.

Clifford the Big Red Dog was not amused and began to suit up. After putting on his big red head, Clifford immediately came to life. I followed him to the lobby, where the extremely animated Clifford began to dance like crazy.

On day two, I was accompanied by an infiltrating partner-in-anthropomorphic-crime who went by the pseudonym "Fluffy." She was also attired in random Halloween costume accessories, including a large bunny nose. Fluffy and I headed toward the "Gofur Room," the operation's brain center, in order to volunteer our services.

"You're not ManBearPig from *South Park*, are you?" asked a volunteer dressed as Napoleon Dynamite.

"Affirmative!" I replied in a robot voice, delighted that someone finally recognized my costume.

Near one of the computers, a commotion broke out. "Is that a zombie penis?" exclaimed a rather intense woman adorned in a black robe. Excited, she leaned in for a closer look at the monitor. "It is a zombie penis!"

Unamused, we decided to leave the volunteer work to others and headed to the bustling vendor room and its array of furry related items, which included plush toys and real, sharp knives.

"This is the sword-breaker," said the stringy-haired dealer who was holding a large knife that easily could have severed a furry's head. "Most furries like blades 'cause most furries are drawn with knives or guns in their hand."

Other dealer tables were covered in furry artwork and comic books, including the popular N'Dar the Wolf.

A perky comic book artist from Florida related her furry fascination: "As a child, I thought I had invented it. Years later, my husband was on the Internet and said, 'Look, other people are doing what you do.' As a kid, I used to draw furry kid-type things, like going to school. When I was a teenager, I would have them doing teenage-type things, like going to concerts. Now, I draw things that my husband and I are into."

The artist showed me an illustration of a humanoid/zebra that was graphically giving a hummer to a fully aroused humanoid/giraffe. She smiled. I reluctantly returned the smile.

It was then that I realized that almost every dealer table had an "Adults Only XXX" booklet on display. Some of the furnography displayed gay animals having interspecies sex, including a male lion boning a male zebra. A Post-it Note covered the penetration point. Other furnography depicted a humanoid/Dalmatian—clad in a fireman's outfit—that was wrapped around a stripper pole with it ass sticking out. Like a William Wegman composition gone horribly wrong, "Big Boys Brandishing Boners," which was described as "erotic art," had nearly every animal species imaginable drawn with huge erections.

"All I can say is that our fantasy is just that—a fantasy," explained a furry who went by the name Fur. "The probability that our fantasies will occur is infinitesimally small. So, we compensate by over-representing sexuality in our media."

And overcompensate they did. Directly adjacent to a table of young girls sketching princesses and unicorns for the G-rated *Baby Furs* comic, a furnography artist furiously sketched, in extreme close-up, a disturbing masterpiece: a unicorn being fisted by a humanized horse. I was beginning to understand why the wholesome, fun-loving furries would have preferred the media not focus on this aspect of furry culture.

"The question is—what's sick, what's wrong, and what's the limit?" said AstroCat. "The anthro-thing makes people uncomfortable because we're all taught from an early age that doing it like they do it on the Discovery Channel is something that Grandma wouldn't approve of."

At least Grandma had her limits.

"Drippy dragon is our most popular dildo. It ejaculates a plastic polymer," said the Scottish mad scientist to Fluffy.

"Do you wear them?" a confused Fluffy asked. "Are they meant for men or women?"

Suddenly, the dealer room supervisor interrupted and asked me if I was a member of the media.

After a flat denial, Fluffy and I were escorted out of the dealer room.

By nightfall, hotel rooms were bustling with a cavalcade of furry-themed parties. Outside one of the rooms, a female unicorn grabbed her wolf-companion's ass and planted a kiss on his forehead with her unicorn snout. "Why don't we have thumpty-thumpty in Ron's room?" enticed the unicorn.

In another room, decorated much like an eight-year-old girl's dream bedroom, a party was happening for furries who were really into Care Bears.

"What's your furry scene like?" I asked a Care Bear who was standing by the door.

"It's a lot of drama," he replied.

Then, an emaciated young woman who was wearing Care Bear pajamas and tightly hugging a teddy bear approached the door and threw out a few furry code words before carefully looking us up and down.

"So how long have you been a furry?" she snapped.

"I'm kind of new. Maybe you can show me the ropes?" I replied. "You got the best decorated room in the whole hotel!"

My attempt at flattery didn't work, and she turned to Fluffy for cross-examination: "Did you go to the Million Bunny March?"

Temporarily caught off guard, Fluffy momentarily paused before replying, "Not this year. But I want to go!"

There was whispering, tension, and more teddy bear clutching.

"Look at what they're wearing!" I heard the Care Bear woman whisper to the others, "They're asking the wrong questions." Finally, she asked us, "Are you press?"

Emphatically, we replied in unison, "No!"

Care Bare woman didn't believe us and retorted, "You need a different badge."

Not to be outdone, a wee munchkin of a Care Bear man interjected: "Bye bye! We're going to make sure you can't drink anywhere on this floor!"

Those Care Bare motherfuckers! If ever there were a group in the world that shouldn't be judgmental, I suspect it should have been the ones clutching the Care Bears. But in our furry costumes, we had managed to freak out the freaky people by being too normal.

I found it fascinating that these furries craved mainstream social acceptance but, like angry children, got pissed off when outsiders found interest in the sexual aspect of their culture. The anger of most furries seemed to stem from a dark, unhappy place where reverting to the comforts of childhood had become their unbridled passion. While leaving in shame, I looked to the heavens and wondered: "Why must they discriminate against the media and, most importantly, ostracize ManBearPig?"

## VIRAL VIDEO FANS

**U**NLESS I AGREED TO a specific set of criteria, a formal sit down interview with Connor Franta would not be possible. His publicist was playing hardball. "If we can guarantee a standalone piece on just Connor, I can lock this in," she said.

My goal was to find a YouTube star to follow around at Stream Con NYC—a three-day festival connecting "thousands of fans, creators, brands, and the industry"—and thought, after his publicist randomly sent me a press release, that Franta might be a good place to start. He seemed relatively popular, and I had absolutely no idea why he was popular. With over five and a half million subscribers and more than four million views on his YouTube channel, Franta had amassed a larger following than some television shows.

But thanks to Franta's publicist, who kept throwing out annoying buzzwords, getting close to this YouTube star was proving more difficult than connecting with a world dignitary. "He's trying to put out there that he's a curator and social tastemaker," she said. "Connor wants to promote all the things he's working on because he is so much more than YouTube at this point."

"Uh-huh" I said in agreement, even though I had known who he was for only ten minutes.

"Yeah, I mean, if the headline is going to be 'Viral Star at Stream Con,' that's something we want to avoid," she said. "We're trying to push Connor and his brand."

So, it was either all Connor or no Connor.

Welcome to the world of digital content and social media stars where, thanks to YouTube, niche communities have their own like-minded celebrities.

The big game-changer occurred in 2006 when Google purchased YouTube for over one and a half billion dollars. Coupled with the rise of smart phones and their built-in cameras, suddenly, everyone was "a creator." With over three hundred hours of videos being uploaded to YouTube every minute, the potential number of video stars—spinning the random viral wheel—became limitless. Soon, Google Analytics was determining who should be a star.

As a result of the influx of content and viewership, the do-it-yourself spirit of early content creators was pushed aside by advertisers willing to pay top dollar to YouTube "stars" willing to promote products to their millions of followers. In fact, Forbes now releases an annual list of the top earning YouTube stars, led by gamer DanTDM, who earned sixteen and a half million dollars in 2017 as a result of his nearly seventeen million followers and eleven billion video views.

With this kind of money involved, managers, agents, and, of course, overprotective publicists started trying to mold their YouTube stars into brand names that transcended what originally made them famous.

Despite this promotional machine, it is still rare for YouTube stars to become household names. Only a few have achieved this status, including Justin Bieber, who was discovered by a talent manager via his YouTube videos, and comedian Bo Burnham, who was plucked from his bedroom and thrust into an international tour and Comedy Central special. In 2018, Burnham further parlayed his success into the mainstream by writing and directing his first feature film, the critically acclaimed *Eighth Grade*.

At Stream Con, the top YouTubers had converged to meet their fans. It was like walking into an alternative universe, where little girls shrieked over people who had made low-budget short films in their basements. A long line careened down a corridor, and fans posed for photos with some of their favorite stars. Almost all of the top male YouTubers looked as if they had been snatched out of a boy band—or a Daniel Radcliffe look-a-like convention.

"I'm at Stream Con, and I just met iJustine," said girl, with outstretched arms, who was talking directly into her phone's camera.

I had just arrived at Stream Con and was already starting to get annoyed.

On the display floor were copies of books written by YouTubers. Apparently, every huge YouTube star had published a book, typically a memoir. So much for a later-in-life memoir written to document one's entire life, not just the first twenty-two years. Shrewd publishers obviously saw the artistic merits—and best-selling potential—of a book written by someone with eight million followers. I guess if the next Hemingway had zero YouTube subscribers, they would never be discovered.

"Notes are fine," said one of the personal publicists of Joey Graceffa, who has almost nine million followers and close to two billion views. "But can you limit the recording of audio until we do the sit down interview?"

We were deep in the bowels of the Javits Center, following Graceffa to his Q&A panel. Since I refused to meet the demands of Connor Franta's publicist, I managed to wrangle my way into Graceffa's entourage. Teenage girls screamed at Graceffa as if he were all the Beatles rolled up into one.

Graceffa started his YouTube channel in 2007 while still in high school. After surviving for a couple of years with a mere two hundred thousand followers, his fan count jumped to two million over the course of a year.

"It put a lot of stress on me that I now had this larger audience, and I felt an obligation to keep posting to the standard of the previous videos I was doing," he said.

In addition to his YouTube subscribers, Graceffa has amassed over four million Twitter followers. His popularity led to a book deal: a memoir, *In Real Life*, and a series of young adult novels. He also has a jewelry line.

We stopped, with his posse in tow, for a quick on-camera interview with *People*.

"He's assessable. He's polished. He's perfect for our market," said the *People* correspondent to her colleague. "I feel he's the most interesting person here."

Next, the correspondent asked Graceffa some pressing pre-interview questions.

"When did you dye your hair?"

"Last week," said Graceffa. The YouTube video of Graceffa getting his hair dyed lavender has received almost one and a half million views.

"Have you met any fans yet?"

Graceffa expressed that he had many fans and that he was really excited to meet them.

When it was time for the camera to roll, the questioning from the *People* correspondent got real: "Tell me about your hairstyle. This is a new look for you."

Graceffa replied: "I wanted to try a new style."

While I documented this amazing banter with a series of scribbles in my notebook, the guy in charge of the shoot approached me with an unhappy face. "Who are you with!?" he demanded. "There can be no reporting on this for five days. This is for *People*. This is an exclusive!"

Apparently, *People* wanted to be the first media outlet to break the story about Graceffa's dyed hair.

Before the *People* interview, we were ushered to a fan event at the Vimeo Theatre, which was filled with ecstatic girls between the ages of ten and fifteen.

"So obviously we're here for Joey, iJustine and GloZell," said the moderator. High-pitched screams erupted, hurting my ears.

"Is anyone dressed up like their favorite YouTube star?" the moderator asked.

Numerous hands went up.

As Graceffa walked on stage, the little girls screamed as if someone had just scored a winning World Cup goal.

"Good morning!" said Graceffa to a sea of camera flashes. Perhaps the girls were filming him for their personal YouTube channels.

"HI JOEY!" the audience shouted back in unison.

"How many of you guys want to be creators or already are?" asked the moderator. Once again, all hands went up.

"If you want to be a creator, just start," said Graceffa, providing some astute advice on the topic.

"If you build it, they will come," added GloZell, stressing that opportunities, such as movie parts, would be offered once their traffic numbers reached into the millions.

Since many YouTubers speak directly into the camera when creating content, fans seemed to operate under the illusion that the video stars were talking directly to them. As a result of this perceived intimacy, a strange camaraderie existed between the famous YouTubers and their very young fans.

"At my first VidCon, I felt like I knew who these YouTubers were because I watched their videos," said Graceffa to me earlier in the day. "I almost expected them to know who I was because I watched their videos."

A guy wearing a hoodie and talking on his cell phone then wandered on stage, interrupting the panel.

"Hello?!" exclaimed GloZell, looking mock-shocked. "Where's the security?"

The guy sat down next to the famous YouTubers and then walked off stage.

"Did you know who that was?" asked the moderator.

"Yaaaaaaaa!" screamed the audience.

I didn't recognize him, but he was apparently a well-known YouTuber himself. It was a meta moment: a viral star had crashed a panel of other viral stars in order to make a viral prank video, all while being filmed by the audience, who hoped that their videos of the prank would go viral as well.

"Seeing Joey has been my favorite moment," said a smitten young girl after seeing him live on stage. It topped her other favorite Stream Con moment: meeting Connor Franta. "I went up to Connor, and I asked for a selfie," she informed me. "And I got a selfie with Connor."

She showed me the selfie, and I made an unhappy face, still upset with the fact that Franta's publicist had shunned me.

"Are your dogs viral video stars?" I asked the owner of two mutts dressed in costumes.

"Not video, but Instagram," clarified the owner of Henry and Penny, whose one hundred thousand followers had garnished the pups television commercials and their very own line of doggy treats.

Attention then shifted from Henry and Penny, who were upstaged by the arrival of Jiff, a fluffy Pomeranian with almost nine million Instagram followers.

"I just want to squish it," said an enamored fan.

Once the canine fanfare subsided, it was time for my big interview with Graceffa. One of his publicists gave me the rundown on what I was not allowed to ask him during our one-on-one sit down. The other publicist told me what I needed to include in my interview questions.

"Be sure to ask him about his upcoming projects," he stressed.

So, I asked Graceffa: "What are your upcoming projects?"

He told me, and I nodded in approval.

Throughout the interview, both publicists hovered directly over my shoulder, making sure I stayed on track. It was like having both parents tag along on a first date. I wondered why these publicists were so over-protective of their YouTube star clients whose fame came from spilling out in their daily YouTube videos every minute detail of their personal lives in some sort of self-imposed *Truman Show*.

In an attempt to scoop *People*, I asked Graceffa about his hair and then followed up by asking him to describe his fans.

"I call my fans psychopaths. Mainly because some of them actually are," said Graceffa with a nervous laugh. "I just heard some crazy stories of some [fans] hiring private detectives, finding out where I live, and delivering me letters."

"Does that freak you out?" I asked.

"It does. Yes. I don't like that," he replied, seeming slightly overwhelmed by all of the adulation he had received from YouTube.

Then, my foray into the world of viral video stars took a turn for the better. "Someone dropped out at the last moment. Would you be interested in moderating a fan Q&A?" asked one of the Stream Con organizers. "It would be with Rosanna Pansino. She has the largest baking show on YouTube."

Having never heard of Rosanna Pansino, I quickly researched her on my iPhone and immediately recognized her from a YouTube ad campaign that ran on New York subways. Pansino's YouTube channel, Nerdy Nummies, has over ten million subscribers and nearly two and half billion views. More than just a baker, she often incorporates science into her videos, creating delectables such as a periodical table of elements made out of cupcakes. Pansino's guests have included Neil deGrasse Tyson and Miss Piggy. Plus, she was just plain charming … and funny, with a self-aware sense of humor.

I was sold! It was time to moderate a Q&A with a top YouTube star and gain perspective on what it was like to be on stage in front of exuberant fans.

"The worst is when you get the moms who come up and say, 'I don't know who you are, but my daughter wanted me to buy your book,'" Pansino told me backstage before the Q&A started.

She also expressed possessing a sense of nervousness about being live on stage in front of her fans. "I live in a bubble," she said. "I don't usually leave my kitchen."

Once on stage in front of a room full of moms and little girls, I momentarily panicked as I forgot how to pronounce Pansino's surname. Fearing that I would be booed by little girls for incorrectly uttering the name of their favorite YouTube star, I, instead, enthusiastically said to the crowd: "WHO HAVE YOU COME TO SEE?"

The little girls shouted her name.

"Please welcome, Rosanna Pansiiiiiiiii …" I announced, trailing off her last name when the applause and fanatic screams grew louder.

The Q&A went great as I bantered with Rosanna to laughs and cheers from her adorable fans, to which she had brought the joys of creative, geeky baking.

"You're my hero and inspire me," expressed one of her shy fans.

Pansino burst into tears, realizing that the impact she had on others transcended her home kitchen bubble. Now glad that I had been blown off by Franta's publicist, I wondered to myself, "Connor who?"

# DRUNK SANTAS

I LOOKED AROUND THE packed Lower East Side pub. A sea of loud, drunken bros—clad in Santa suits—downed Tequila shots while naughty, reindeer vixens twerked on top of the bar. None of these revelers would have been there if it weren't for the man I was talking to on my phone.

"Watch out for Santas puking on you," warned John Law, one of the original organizers of SantaCon back in 1994. "I haven't done this event since 1998. I haven't put on a vomit-encrusted Santa suit in quite a while. We were just kind of done with it back then."

Much like everything else that innocently starts with good intentions, SantaCon began as a vastly different subversive beast than it has become. At its onset, the founders had no idea that their event would devolve into the drunken and loathed monstrosity that I was witnessing. "I have mixed feelings about the direction the event has taken," said Law. New Yorkers don't; they fear the beard.

Each year, with the flair of a Santa-suited amateur night, over thirty thousand people take to the streets of New York for the holiday-themed booze fest. And quicker than a sloshed Santa can say, "Onward Dancer and Prancer," the costumed mentality of the mass mob gives St. Nick revelers and merrymakers a license to behave badly. During SantaCon, it has become commonplace to see shit-faced Santas brawling, vomiting, urinating, and pleasuring each other in public. Before noon, I had already walked by a Santa pissing on the door of a church in my neighborhood.

"We had no intention of creating some giant, stupid wave of marauding crimson that was going to sweep across the planet," said Law about SantaCon's origins. The catalyst for the very first event was inspired by the Danish performance/activist group Solvognen. In 1974, that theater troupe took en masse to the streets of Copenhagen and pulled many wacky antics, such as taking items directly off of department store shelves and giving them as presents to customers—that is until security whisked them away.

"It's kind of weird being involved with these things and seeing them blow up through the Internet," said Law, who also had a hand in starting another mega-cultural event: Burning Man. SantaCon has now spread worldwide to almost four hundred cities in over fifty countries. "It kind of still blows my mind."

The first SantaCon was just one of many events put on by the San Francisco Cacophony Society, a "randomly gathered network of individuals united … through subversion, pranks, art, fringe explorations and meaningless madness." Organized by newsletter—when social media was still science fiction—as a one-time event, it unfolded organically as a subversive culture-jam to protest holiday consumerism and take back Christmas from Macy's, Coca-Cola, and Jesus.

"We had thirty-three Santas, and the event was perfect," recalled Law. "It was shocking! It created that momentary mind-fuck of 'What's going on here?' People's jaws were literally hanging open."

Interactions with the public were intended to be funny and amiable. Santas marched through Macy's yelling, "Charge it," and had a spontaneous snowball fight with kids at a public skating rink. Booze played no role in the original Santa mayhem.

"The Cacophony philosophy was to try not to be dicks when doing events," Law said.

However, the inaugural SantaCon was not intended to resemble a Hallmark Christmas special. "We pushed the limits ... a lot," recalled Law. "I got hanged by the neck as Santa. That's pretty shocking. It's not like we were angels or anything."

With a body harness hidden under his Santa suit, Law capped the SantaCon evening by donning a noose around his neck and hanging himself from a traffic light. It was pure performance art. "We waited until midnight to do that. There weren't any kids on the street when that happened," Law said, stressing the Cacophony Society ethos.

When SantaCon returned the following year, the group had grown to one hundred Santas. Even though the philosophy remained the same ("act Santa-like"), things got out of the control: three Santas were arrested after crashing a débutante ball at San Francisco's Fairmont Hotel.

"Santa Robert swiped a bottle of Sky vodka and drank the whole thing over the course of a half-hour," Law recalled. "He ended up projectile vomiting on the bus. That was the first vomiting I knew of."

As the Internet grew in popularity, so did SantaCon. As word of the event spread across the web, splinter groups formed in other cities. As a result, in 1996 the Cacophony Society brought SantaCon to Portland, Oregon, where the local police were so frazzled at the arrival of a multitude of Santas that they deployed hundreds of cops to tail the Clauses, who they believed to be a violent threat.

According to Law, police handed out to every business in downtown Portland official memos that read: "Anarchists dressed as Santa will try to trash your businesses this weekend. Please be aware of them."

Law thought, "You got to be kidding me."

With the police unnecessarily outfitted in full riot gear, Law advised participants: "You can't get mad at them; you're fucking Santa. You can't get mad and yell, 'Fuck off cops,' because this is not what that's about ... and it will totally fuck everything up."

Fortunately, no one was arrested. The Santas simply crashed a roller rink and then sang Christmas carols at a mall.

When SantaCon first came to New York in 1998, the agenda was to have a "shit-ton of Santas" climb the rocks in Central Park and flash-mob popular Christmas spots, such as Saks Fifth Avenue, the Plaza Hotel, and the Christmas tree at Rockefeller Center.

"I don't remember any incidents at all. I think we stopped at two or three bars maybe," Law said. Most of the events were centered on creative subversiveness. "We went to the United Nations, and we made protest posters with things like: 'UN Out of North Pole, No More Reindeer Games.' They were goofy posters. And we protested for fifteen to twenty minutes."

During the inaugural New York SantaCon, a true Christmas moment occurred after the mass of Santas descended on the Lake at Central Park, where roughly one hundred people were ice skating. "All these ice skaters stopped skating, and they started cheering. And we were waving and going, 'Ho-ho-ho!'" Law reminisced. "For me, as a guy who hated Christmas, I got teary-eyed. I got choked up. I thought, 'Wow, this is really cool.' I actually got the Christmas spirit for a moment."

That Christmas spirit continued as Law and a Detroit Santa climbed the cables of the Brooklyn Bridge and then followed all the Santas to a Goth club in the Meatpacking District, where they danced the merry night away. Ho-ho-ho!

It was trying to capture this type of Christmas joy that motivated Law to start SantaCon. "When I was nine, I realized that Santa Claus was a lie, and it was really hurtful," said Law. "When you're a kid and you realize that Santa Claus doesn't exist, nobody talks about it. It's the beginning of your indoctrination into middle-class hypocrisy. I didn't like Christmas after that."

Creating SantaCon, thereby, gave Law a new reason to celebrate. "We could take Christmas back and make it a fun holiday event instead of a hypocritical excuse for filling the pockets of Macy's," Law said. "That was part of my motivation, because I'm horrified by that commercial hypocrisy and that Jesus Christ myth and all the other bullshit that goes along with it. Doing this event—and having that response—was a way of going, 'Hey! This is our party. It's our

Christmas too!'"

But SantaCon now exists in a parallel universe, where protests of commercialism have been replaced by a massive, day-long pub-crawl that climaxes with an evening of people throwing up on the subway, which was why I, like many members of the press, showed up for the event. As if we were paparazzi trying to capture a shitfaced celebrity emerging from a nightclub, members of the media wanted shocking photos of drunken Santas spilling out of bars and puking in the streets of New York.

"If you're going to puke, then puke responsibly," said a man to a press videographer. "'Cause that's what people want to see. They want to see the puke, and they want to see the handjobs."

No wonder Law has mixed feelings about the beast he created. So do most New Yorkers, especially the "real" Santas directly affected by the current state of the event. Take Glen Heroy, a professional Santa who, for the last thirty years, has portrayed the jolly one during the holiday season. He feels great hostility towards SantaCon.

"My Santa rig cost upward of three thousand dollars," Heroy said. "So, when I'm leaving a gig and need to catch a cab to my next gig, and it happens to be during SantaCon, no cab will stop for me. I find I am a victim of a strange kind of profiling from taxi drivers. And as the tenth vacant cab that passes me by, I want to shout: 'I'm not like them! I'm a real Santa!'"

For Law, a turning point occurred several years ago when he totally forgot the event was happening. He walked out of his San Francisco apartment and nearly tripped over a Santa-suited college kid who was vomiting on his steps. Later that day, he cringed as a group of drunken Santas were being thrown out of his favorite neighborhood café.

"I felt really bad," Law said. "Kind of like, 'Fuck! This is what happened!?'" He told me that he saw the bastardization of the event as some sort of karmic payback.

"The Santa-thing ... we didn't plan this. But it's all over the place," he said. "Some of them are probably straight-up frat bro beer fests. And some of them are probably more interesting. Who knows? I'm not going to give it a value judgment, but it's definitely interesting. Beyond that, if the whole idea is just to get shit-faced drunk, and that's all they're doing, then that's kind of dumb. It's kind of boring."

Law was dumbfounded when he learned how massive the New York SantaCon had become. "Thirty thousand! It blew my mind. I had no idea. I'm not against it, and I'm not for it. I'm ambivalent," he said. "I actually wouldn't mind seeing thirty thousand Santas … from a distance. Just the image is so overwhelming. Of course it's fucking amazing. I mean, how can it not be amazing."

While SantaCon, from its noble origins, may have turned in to a drunken shit-show loathed by local residents, Law said he can still appreciate the anarchy of mass Santas rampaging through a city. "If you want to have a public gathering in a society that is rapidly becoming a police state, there's some power there … there's some value in that," added Law. "The flip side of that is there's no thought involved. But I had fun doing it. I'm glad I did it … but I'm kind of over it."

# FOR
# CHRIST'S SAKE

### TRIBES
Hookers for Jesus
Jump for Jesus
Body-slammin' for Jesus

### TRIBAL LEADERS
Pastor Benny / Annie Lobert
Gene "Sully" Sullivan
Dr. Shock / Rob Adonis

### WHERE TO SPOT TRIBE MEMBERS
Church of South Las Vegas / The Strip
Where the Lord Wants Them to Be
Churches and Skating Rinks in Rural Georgia

### TRIBAL TRAITS
Walking the Streets for the Lord
Jumping Through Walls of Fire
Wearing Ridiculously Tight Costumes

# HOOKERS FOR JESUS

THE SPIRITUAL JOINT WAS packed for the Saturday night church service, Vegas-style: purple lights in retro 1970s circles, a rock band on the pulpit, and videos. Everyone was on their feet and clapping to the music. It was plain rowdy—holy church-style.

"Are you scared yet?" whispered Annie Lobert.

"No. Why?" I asked.

"You're sitting in church with a row of hookers," she joked.

Annie filled me in on Houston, the gorgeous blond woman sitting next to me. "We used to work together," she said. "We had the same pimp."

Other sex workers in attendance included pint-sized Destiny, who was pregnant with her pimp's baby; Roxy, a big-boned woman with angular, penciled-in eyebrows; and Starr, a nineteen-year-old ex-prostitute, who sang in the choir.

"She used to be a sex worker, too," said Annie, referring to a red-headed woman in a black dress. The former street walker offered a warm "hello" as she passed by. "Now she has a good job with a hotel."

After having mixed results at several other churches, Hookers for Jesus finally found a home at the Church of South Las Vegas. "This church really embraced the ministry," declared Annie. "Pastor Benny and Wendy have a huge heart for prostitutes."

Annie was raised in Minnesota as a churchgoing, goody two-shoes. At age eighteen, her life changed when after a chance encounter with a pimp she was "turned out" into the sex industry. For eleven years, Annie lived in Satan's fiery fast lane, selling her body, turning tricks, cavorting with celebrities, and hobnobbing with drug dealers. As a high-priced Vegas escort, she earned up to five hundred dollars per hour.

The call girl lifestyle, however, took its toll on Annie. Drug addiction claimed most of her earnings, and she was forced to live in her car. But a moment of clarity arrived with a shocking jolt: Annie overdosed on cocaine and suffered a massive heart attack. Then, she turned her life back to Jesus and looked to him for guidance.

Reborn as a woman of faith, Annie formed Hookers for Jesus to bring salvation to other women trapped in prostitution.

"During the time I was a prostitute, I thought God hated me," she said. "People said, 'You'll be nothing but a hooker the rest of your life.'" Annie's new calling—getting prostitutes off the streets and hooked on church—aims to prove them wrong.

And prove them wrong she did. Annie not only found the Almighty but also a husband: Oz Fox, the guitarist from everyone's favorite 1980s spandex-clad, Christian metal band—Stryper.

"The hired hand runs away from the sheep 'cause he's only in it for the money," preached Pastor Benny, the amiable church leader with an offbeat sense of humor. Live sheep in cages, which were positioned right on the pulpit, heckled Pastor Benny.

"How many people are involved in the sex industry?" Pastor Benny asked the congregation. In my vicinity, all hands went up.

Directing his attention to the row of hookers, Pastor Benny continued: "Annie Lobert was one of the top call girls in the Valley. Her name in the industry was Fallen. If I can save Annie Lobert, I can save anyone!"

After the service, Annie light-heartedly joked with churchgoers:

"Look at Janice wearing those hooker shoes."

Houston seemed inspired. "I used to think, 'When I get myself together, I'll come.' I didn't want to be a hypocrite," she recalled. "But it was killing me. I had to be whacked out drunk to work."

Eventually, Houston heeded to Pastor Benny's advice: "Don't clean up first. No. Come to Christ, and he'll change your nature from the inside!"

Despite the loss of income, Houston stopped lap dancing and giving "extras" on the side. "I'd be making three thousand dollars a weekend. Now, I'm broke as a joke, but I'm happy. And I'm peaceful," she said. "I just want to find a good guy."

As the spiritually charged congregation continued to exit into the warm Las Vegas night, Pastor Benny said, "As far as we know, we're the only church in the Valley to have a house (Destiny House) for ex-prostitutes. Hookers for Jesus—that would scare a lot of pastors."

Not only does it scare other pastors, the existence of Hookers for Jesus also has led to Christian-bashing from other Christians. "They say we're false prophets," added Annie. "They don't believe Jesus in his true form, which is non-judgmental, loving, helping people."

In spite of this criticism from other Christians, both Annie and Pastor Benny remain unfazed in their mission. "If you can do it for those four girls, you can do it for another four," stressed Pastor Benny. "Our church can spark other churches to open up a home. Little by little, we're seeing girl's lives change. It's not like *Pretty Woman*."

Located in a quiet, nondescript suburban neighborhood, Destiny House provides safe housing for ex-prostitutes who have escaped the industry. At the time of my visit, it was home to three ex-prostitutes and their children. One of the women, Sonja, went from earning big money while hooking to working at a coffee shop for minimum wage. Living with her at Destiny House were her two toddlers, a boy and a girl, both of whom were fathered by her pimp. Sonja's daughter was sick with a hacking cough.

"When a girl leaves a pimp, she loses everything," explained Annie.

Inside the comfortable duplex, baby toys were scattered on the floor, and finger paintings hung on the refrigerator.

Another tenant, Destiny, turned to prostitution at the age of seventeen after being disowned by her father, a prominent community official. "You'll be there in the delivery room, right?" she asked Annie with almost childlike innocence. Annie assured Destiny that she would be there.

Sonja went upstairs with Roxy, the house's third tenant, to get ready for the night's casino outreach. Starr, the nineteen-year-old ex-prostitute, had come over to babysit.

Annie was dressed stylishly for the casino outreach. "It makes me realistic to the girls," said Annie. "It's who I am."

The plan for the evening was to meet with working girls at casinos and provide them with colorful and neatly wrapped gift bags filled with niceties such as lip moisturizer, vanilla splash body spray, lotion, a scented candle, perfume, an invitation to church, and, of course, the Bible.

"Girly stuff," Annie said. "It's everything they need so they can later take a bath and read the Bible!"

Making the outreach night extra-special was the fact that it was also Annie's forty-second birthday. "I want to spend my birthday giving back to the girls," she said. "Jesus got to serve. I want to serve."

Before we piled into Annie's car, Starr led a short prayer. Everyone bowed their heads. As we departed the quiet suburban neighborhood, the ex-prostitutes reverted to their tough-talking, street-smart personas.

"Treasure Island's a good place to start. There's a lot of hos," informed Sonja.

"I'm not going to Fremont Street unless we have a gun. It's full of ghetto pimps and circuit girls," said Roxy.

"She's nervous that we might run into her ex-pimp," added Annie.

In a recent downtown visit, the women had an encounter with a twenty-one-year-old pimp who harassed them for over an hour. "He was like, 'What's you all doing? What's up? What's up? You know what time it is!? It's pimp time!'" said Roxy, mimicking the pimp.

"He had a big tattoo on his neck saying he's the King," added Annie. "I told him, 'You ain't the King. The King is Jesus! You have a gift that you use for evil gain. You should use it for Jesus.'"

Fortunately, that episode ended peacefully. "We could tell he was rolling off of ecstasy. His eyes in his head were black," said Roxy. "It's really not advisable to get mouthy to a pimp. They can pull out a gun or knife or throw you down to the floor."

As the flashing casino lights of Las Vegas Boulevard neared, the women talked about shoes and the money they once made inside the casinos. "I've been eighty-sixed from every hotel on the strip," proclaimed Annie, who recalled once being kicked out by security in front of the *Wizard of Oz* shop while drunk and high on coke.

Inside the parking garage of the New York-New York Hotel and Casino, we unloaded the gift bags into an inconspicuous sack as Annie planned our strategy. "If security catches us, we'll get kicked out for soliciting," informed Annie. "We won't stay in one place very long."

Before starting our mission, Annie playfully declared, "We got you Harmon. You're with three Hookers for Jesus!"

Inside the casino, we trolled the slot machine area, where round-bellied tourists pulled at levers like Pavlovian zombies questing for biscuits of clanking gratification. Drunken men leered as Roxy eyed the crowd for possible targets. "Lately, everyone looks like they're ho-ing," she remarked, commenting on the hooker-like fashion sense of the typical female Vegas reveler.

Pointing to a casino worker dressed as a showgirl, I asked, "Is that one?"

Ignoring my failed attempt at humor, Annie mentioned that approximately ninety percent of prostitutes operate "undercover," bypassing the casino floor and, instead, going directly to hotel rooms. It makes Annie's job more difficult. "Some nights we'll see forty girls. Some nights we'll see only three," she said.

"Have you ever approached the wrong person?" I asked as a group of trashy tourists—that to the untrained eye could have passed as prostitutes—walked by.

"Usually we're dead on," she said. "But these outreaches are unpredictable. Sometimes the girls are very responsive. Sometimes nothing."

For example, when a potential target says, "Fuck you, you fucking bitch. I'm not working," it means that they are working. Or if someone emphatically says, "I'm not a hooker," it definitely means that they are a hooker. "Some girls don't want to admit it," added Annie. "It hurts their ego."

Sonja found a possible target: a curly-haired and worn-looking woman wearing a short—and extremely tight—pink dress and pumps. She was sitting alone at a slot machine and raised her eyebrows every time a man passed by.

"How can you be sure?" I asked.

"She's waiting on her own with a sense of purpose," Annie explained.

Without hesitation, Annie approached the woman, and a friendly conversation ensued. After receiving her complimentary gift bag, the hooker disappeared into a melee of drunken tourists, roulette wheels, and potential tricks and Johns.

"I just told her God loves her," Annie said. "And since God loves you, then you don't have to do this."

I asked Annie if she thought the woman would come to church.

"I think so," she replied. "She looked tired."

As we left New York-New York for Excalibur, Annie was approached by a clean-cut guy who was handing out promotional cards for a bar. "Oh my God! You're the Hooker for Jesus girl!" he exclaimed. "My wife was in jail, and you guys gave her one of your cards. You said you'd pray for her."

Following a brief conversation with the man, the prostitute hunting resumed. "Look at her. She's totally working it," said Annie of a prostitute who looked like an Art Crumb cartoon. "That's old school. She has it all hanging out. She's so 1999."

Next, Annie spotted a young hooker sitting with two guys by the beer pong tables. "She's green, too. Look how she's acting," said

Annie.

"Are you going to move in with a gift bag?" I asked.

"If a girl is with a client, you don't want to wreck their game," replied Annie. "They'll just get pissed and say, 'Why are you trying to mess up my money?'"

Roxy added, "You don't want to wreck what she's doing. Maybe she's got a quota."

An African American man in a white suit and a Kangol hat moved about the bar like a shark circling its prey. "Roxy said that's a pimp she knows named Marvin," informed Annie before approaching a stunning blond woman in a tight purple dress. The pair immediately connected, sharing laughs and possibly a few hair tips. After a several minutes, Annie brought the woman to me for introductions. "She's a police officer in Sweden!" exclaimed Annie.

"I'm here for the body building convention!" said the woman. Then, she explained how prostitution is dealt with in Sweden: "We arrest the Johns to crack down on the demand."

Although the casino seemed pretty hooker-packed to me, by one in the morning Sonja was ready to leave. "It's a slow night," she said.

On our way out, Roxy pointed out a stocky, undercover vice cop who was sitting alone at the bar nursing a drink. "They always look a little too clean cut," she said. "Or they try to look touristy but not touristy."

Outside, the Metro Police—sporting bright yellow jackets—had detained two very young prostitutes.

"Why did they stop these two when the entire Strip is swarming with prostitutes?" I asked.

"They just rolled someone maybe?" hypothesized Annie. "Or possibly, security sees them every night for two weeks coming and going, riding up and down the elevator all night. They're just harassing them."

With a glint in her eye, Annie saw the young prostitutes as an incarnation of her former self. "When I used to do this by myself, it was crazy because I had no one to protect me," said Annie, recalling her first outreach. "I just wanted to save them."

## JUMP FOR JESUS

THE FLAMES FROM THE eight-foot wall crawled thirty feet high as temperatures soared to almost two thousand degrees. "That represents the Gates of Hell, which Jesus said stands in the way between God and eternity," announced Gene "Sully" Sullivan to the crowd. "All the darkness activity blinds us to eternity, and that's what the wall represents. Those gates prevent people from seeing into eternity and prevent those who are gone from extending into paradise."

Sully, the motorcycle daredevil and former bodyguard of Evel Knievel, had a spiritual awakening and now does all his motorcycle stunts for the Lord. Since 1978, he's been jumping through walls of fire in the name of Jesus Christ. For Sully, a miracle is just a jump away.

"This probably won't fly in your local church, but the fact is the Lord sent me to Evel Knievel," Sully told me. "The Lord created that whole thing. More people have received and heard the message of Jesus Christ because of Evel Knievel—and me being his first bodyguard—than anything I could've done on my own."

The seventy-one-year-old Sully, who, according to Guinness World Records, is the oldest and longest active motorcycle stunt rider, said that he owes his journey to Jesus through years spent with Knievel, the hard-living stunt rider who adorned himself in a red, white, and blue jumpsuit.

But before turning his life towards the Lord's angels, Sully, thanks to Knievel, had a life-changing rendezvous with the Hells Angels biker gang. A professional bodyguard at the time, Sully first met Knievel in 1970 when he tagged along with his dad, a prominent San Francisco sports writer, who was assigned to interview Knievel about his jump at the Cow Palace, an indoor arena in Daly City, California. Long before Johnny Knoxville's antics in *Jackass* and the arrival of the X Games, Knievel, the ultimate motorcycle showman, set the extreme sports standard, crashing more than twenty times and suffering over four hundred bone fractures.

"My dad asked me to go with him because he didn't know what the guy was like," recalled Sully. "I stayed and had several beers with Knievel, and he asked me if I'd come to the Cow Palace the next night to help him out."

Sully agreed, which proved a good thing: that evening Knievel was jumped by the Hells Angels.

"The announcer was half-in-the-bag that night and said, 'If Evel Knievel makes this jump, he'll set the Hells Angels back one hundred years.' Obviously, they were in the crowd, and that was not the right thing to say."

In the 1970s, the Hells Angels gained notoriety after beating up hippy concertgoers and stabbing a man to death at the Altamont Speedway Free Festival, where they were hired by the Rolling Stones to provide security.

"A Hells Angel threw a wrench at Knievel on his way up the takeoff ramp," recalled Sully. "It didn't hit him. He made the jump and came back around."

While Knievel completed his victory lap around the track, the Hells Angels flooded the infield and waited for him to return. Of course, a melee ensued. Knievel leaped off of his bike, and the Hells Angels threw him to the ground like a rag doll. In true badass fashion, Sully ran across the infield at top speed and smashed full-force into the Hells Angels. As the crowd jumped in to the fray to back up their hero, Sully grabbed Knievel and hauled him to safety right before a full-blown ruckus broke out.

"I just plowed into a bunch of them and got Knievel out of there," said Sully. And thanks to the die-hard Evel Knievel fans, "They took every single one of the Hells Angels to the hospital."

Sully immediately became Knievel's bodyguard and went on the road with him as his right-hand man. "Any sane person would've backed out after the Hells Angels deal," said Sully with a laugh. "Evel was concerned that they would go after him. But we never had any encounters with them after that."

Those bodyguard days served as Sully's apprenticeship into becoming a motorcycle daredevil. "I had a motorcycle, but I really didn't consider doing stunts or anything like that before meeting Knievel," he said.

But soon, Sully had mastered his own stunts, including jumping over fifty five-gallon drums into a burning wall. He learned the most by watching Knievel's mistakes. For example, Knievel once crashed and broke his shoulder after attempting to jump thirteen cars. Had he listened to Sully, who advised him to adjust the position of the landing ramp rather than moving the takeoff ramp back in order to clear the additional cars, the stunt would have proceeded without incident.

In 1972, as a favor to a friend, Sully went to a Christian Fellowship breakfast, which led to his biggest leap of them all: a leap of faith into the land of the Holy. "The Lord just really encountered me at that meeting," Sully said. "Really nothing like that happened to me before.

"For forty minutes, the Lord was speaking in my heart and showing me my life, my sins, my whole lifestyle. I walked out of that place changed."

As a result of his spiritual encounter, Sully did a three-sixty on his fast lane lifestyle, including turning his back on a two million dollar movie contract. "If I would've gone that way, the Lord wouldn't be in anything I did. It would have been just me," he said. "When you meet 'The Man,' that changes everything."

Sully also severed ties with Knievel. "My biggest issue with being Knievel's bodyguard: I was having to defend him from the good guys, because he's the guy creating all the problems. He's the guy out there that's being the jerk," recalled Sully. "We'd go into a nightclub or a bar, and he's loud. He's boisterous. He's after the women. He'd offer to buy everyone a drink, but he's just being a jerk. He's taking over. He's telling people what to do. You know, not cool.

"I had to stand between him and the local good guys who were like, 'Hey, why don't you take your fame and go somewhere else.' I didn't feel comfortable with that. That didn't happen a lot, but that happened enough."

Despite Sully's come-to-Jesus moment, Knievel still tried in 1974 to coax him into assisting with the legendary Snake River Canyon jump, which ended in failure.

"The fact is—I backed off. I told him I came to the Lord. I'm not doing this," said Sully. "It highly offended him."

Instead, Sully allowed divine intervention, via the hand of Jesus, to change his motorcycle stunt show. Using the flaming-motorcycle-aerial-knowledge set he gained while working for Knievel, Sully interconnected his jumps to the Bible, soaring selflessly for what later would later become Jump for Jesus.

"I'd been jumping through this burning wall, which didn't make a lot of sense," Sully explained. "But when I came to the Lord, I saw the burning wall as the Gates of Hell. And the Lord helped me put an analogy of the jump together that is a tremendous message."

The Jump for Jesus rally started with Sully explaining to the crowd, which neared four hundred people, the true spiritual meaning behind his jump. "The takeoff ramp represents our launch into life—so we become accountable for what we do. We've launched off the takeoff ramp of life, and we're headed somewhere," he said. "The gap represents the darkness and pitfalls of this life.

"Whatever the darkness is, that's the gap we're jumping. We're going through life, and the object is to stay above the darkness and not … be consumed by it."

Then, it was time for the motorcycle ministry climax, where Sully was to smash through an eight-foot firewall that had been doused with five gallons of gasoline. He informed the crowd that if they agreed with the word of God, then they would pass through the Gates of Hell, much like his flying motorcycle would pass through the wall of fire. If they didn't agree, then, well, they should expect a fiery eternity.

"When I break through that wall and I come through the other side, the landing ramp has a big white cross on it and that represents eternal life," said Sully.

Motorcycle dexterity, fire, and Jesus dazzled the spectators. After the jump, all were invited to pray with Sully and his crew, who were clad in "Team Jesus" T-shirts. Souls were saved, autographs were signed, and free barbecue was devoured.

Every spring, Sully and his right-hand man depart their home base of Billings, Montana in search of towns to bring their motorcycle stunt ministry. "We're old school. We go out and look where we want to go," Sully shared. "When we find a community that we feel the Lord wants us to be in, we start promoting."

To date, his greatest performance was jumping for ten thousand people in the South Pacific. Sully and his team of twenty people traveled to a remote island, where they were treated like spiritual rock stars. "The King of Tonga invited me to come and do Jump for Jesus for his seventy-ninth birthday," Sully said. "I jumped in a corridor of people. It was absolutely electric!"

Jump for Jesus' most publicized event occurred in 2008 in Blanchester, Ohio. A local pastor organized the jump in order to get people into his church. In the name of the Lord, Sully soared his motorcycle over the world's largest horseshoe crab—thirty feet long with a twenty-five-foot-long upraised spiky tail—and through the fiery Gates of Hell.

"Do you find it a religious experience, when you're actually in the air?" I asked Sully, wondering if he felt guided by a spiritual hand that helped lift him and his motorcycle through the wall of fire.

"No!" Sully chuckled. "I just pay attention to what I'm doing."

Evidently, it was all hard work—Sully practices up to fifteen jumps before each Jump for Jesus program—with no divine intervention.

"I used to do some really wild stuff," said Sully about some of his early stunts, including his 1972 World Record in which he jumped a Triumph 500 equipped with skis one hundred eighty feet into a lake.

"Afterwards, the Lord got a hold of me and said, 'Look, you do what you can do safely. If you can jump the ten cars safely, then do it.' But he said, 'If you can't, and you put eleven in there, then you own the eleventh car,'" added Sully with a laugh. "The Lord says don't push it so much. Fame and glory is what kills everybody. It either kills you slowly through vice, or it kills you rapidly through some harebrained idea that snuffs your life."

Finally, I asked Sully the obvious question: "Did you ever try to spread the message of the Lord to Evel Knievel?"

Sully chuckled before replying, "Oh, yeah, but he wasn't interested back then at all. The guy was a whoremonger. He was a liar, a drunk. Obviously, he never got drunk before he jumped. The guy held it together, but you know, his off-life was terrible."

But in 2007, Evel Knievel, according to Sully, had his own personal encounter with Jesus. Their friendship came full circle when a Born Again Evel phoned him and told him of the Devil, saying "You bastard, get away from me and never come back!"

Sully claimed Knievel was a changed man. "He had a legitimate encounter, and that November, he passed," said Sully."

He admitted that in life, Knievel's message was great, especially his outreach to kids about not doing drugs. "He had some great things to say, but he didn't walk the talk. His life was a total contradiction to his words and his message," Sully said. "The Lord led me to the man. I served him and learned from him. And the great thing is—at the end of his life, we reconnected. And he understood my decision."

Although the two ended up taking vastly different life paths, the very last jump Knievel ever saw was Sully doing Jump for Jesus at his annual stunt celebration in Butte, Montana.

"He told me it was the best program at Evel Knievel Days that year," said Sully. "He loved it. He absolutely loved it!"

# BODY-SLAMMIN' FOR JESUS

**D**R. SHOCK, THE GOOD-OL'-BOY ring announcer, asked the crowd, "Are you ready for some good old fashion wrasslin'?" Hungry for wresting excitement, they responded with cheers and applause. The bell rang, and an overweight wrestler known as Mr. Evil flew off the ropes, delivering a crushing hangman's neck breaker to his unfortunate opponent, Dixie Dynamite.

"Come on Dixie, come on!" screamed a chubby redheaded kid.

Ka-pow! Dixie was leveled in the back of the head with a metal folding chair. As they carried his body out of the wrestling ring, Dr. Shock, who stood on stage in front of a large wooden cross, said to the hardened wrestling fans, "Hey, how many people love Jesus Christ?"

It was a typical Saturday night in rural Georgia, where wrestling is religion—literally! At the Harvest Church, body-slammin' for Jesus was the ultimate battle of good versus evil.

Inside the dressing room, bare-chested Christian wrestlers donned in spandex tights wrapped their wrists with tape and grabbed each other, practicing ring moves that had been crafted with biblical symbolism in mind. "He's going to hit me. I'm going to land on my back, and we're going to call that move the Fallen Angel," instructed Rob Adonis, the founder of Ultimate Christian Wrestling (UCW).

This perfect marriage of Christianity and WWE-style wrestling was resurrected by Adonis in June 2003. "Our first show was in Canton, Georgia—at a skating rink. We packed out the place. About two hundred people were there," he explained. "We had three people that made a move and were saved that night."

After spending five years in mainstream wrestling, inspiration for UCW struck Adonis in the middle of the night. "I woke up on my birthday in a cold sweat," he said. "I felt I had something laid on me to do. It's been a stellar ride ever since."

UCW spreads its wrestling gospel of Jesus all over the state of Georgia. "Typically, in every show, ten percent of the crowd will make a move to give their life to Christ," Adonis said. "So, if we have a hundred in the crowd, ten people will move. And that's what we're going for. It's the folks that don't know Christ, that don't have any idea about salvation or forgiveness of sin. That's the one's we're really trying to go after."

As the rowdy crowd filed in to the church and took their seats in metal folding chairs, a DJ spun Christian rock music, setting the spiritual tone for the high-flying, body-slamming action that was about to commence. At the concession stand, popular items included *Where the Big Boys Pray* T-shirts and other impulse wrestling swag such as the Bible. Hordes of small children scurried about the auditorium, waiting restlessly for their favorite grapplers to take the ring.

Since UCW falls in to the category of independent Christian wrestling, the athletes range in size from muscled with big pot bellies ("heels") to scrawny skinny kids ("baby-faces") who wrestle in street clothes.

"We got characters at this point that have gotten so much popularity that they've got a following," expounded Adonis. "And these people, collectively, they will find people that won't go to church … but they go to wrestling shows. And they come in and meet Christ. It's a life changing experience."

Between matches, the adrenaline-filled wrestlers gathered in the dressing room for a prayer. Mr. Evil, Dustin Powers, Frankie Valentine, and Dixie Dynamite—all in their ridiculous wrestling outfits—bowed their heads. "Thank you God for letting us do what we enjoy," prayed Adonis. "We're doing all this for you and your kingdom, God …"

But not everyone agrees that it is a good idea to mix the pacifist message of Christ with the violence of hitting people on the head with metal folding chairs. While putting on a karate robe, Adonis shared with the group an encounter he had with a pastor who frowned upon the idea of Christian wrestling.

"He told me, 'Everyone at our church is already saved, and we want to keep it that way!' Man, I got to get a copy of that Bible he's using," Adonis said with a laugh. "Wow, does God win in his Bible, too?!"

Plus, there were a few moments that, understandably, raised some Christian eyebrows.

"Every woman's dream," announced Dr. Shock, "Frankie Valentine. LET'S MAKE SOME NOISE!" The crowd went wild as Valentine appeared in the ring with the outline of his large package clearly visible in his tight tights, leaving nothing for the Christian imagination.

Adonis assured me that the costume was biblically accurate. "There were men in the Bible who dressed up in loin clothes and ran through the marketplace all in the name of Christ," he said. "Our philosophy is to get them in here. Do whatever you got to do, and give them the truth. The truth will set them free. You know, that's our goal."

So, the sexually explicit clothing can be explained away as biblical. But what about the gratuitous violence and all the blood?

"We try to avoid the blood," Adonis explained. "It happens on accident, yeah. We always have chairs flying. I've had my nose busted open a couple of times from some miscues. The crowd goes crazy. People like gore."

After a moment, taking a more Christian approach, Adonis added, "We don't like blood, because one, it's not real sanitary. Two, we don't like to mar up our mat; we like to keep it all nice and clean. And three, most churches don't want to see it; the kids don't want to see it. So, if there's any blood, it's purely because there's something sticking out of the chair, and boom, it hits you and rips you open."

Before the main event, which was billed as the Ultimate Showdown, I sat down with announcer Dr. Shock, who has done it all in the wrestling business, including running American All Pro-Wrestling.

"I was in the mainstream. I was being booked in bars, mountain homes, and trailer parks. If there's a place to put a wrestling ring, I've put one there," he said.

"What made you tire of the mainstream?" I asked.

"Just the vulgarity, the alcohol, the cursing ... stuff you'd associate with wrestling nowadays. When I got redirected in church and to Jesus, it was hard for me to go out Saturday night."

As a result, Dr. Shock sold his wrestling organization and gave himself to the heavyweight champ of all-time: Jesus Christ.

"What's the big difference between UCW and the WWE?" I asked him.

"The WWE, that's a whole different realm, a whole different realm," replied Dr. Shock. "I don't even watch that stuff on TV. Mainly it's based on how big the guy can be and how good looking the lady can be. It has nothing to do with Jesus ... in my opinion."

Finally, it was time for the main event. "Hey, I just got to say something," announced Dr. Shock. "How many people love Jesus Christ?"

As the crowed responded with applause and cheers, Mr. Evil—clad in dark shades, a trench coat, and carrying the heavyweight belt on his shoulder—entered the ring to a cloud of smoke and Drowning Pool's "Let the Bodies Hit the Floor," which blared over the church's sound system. The cheers and applause quickly morphed into boos, jeers, and taunts.

"Go home!" heckled someone from the crowd. Mr. Evil, in the

most un-Christian way possible, told the man to shut up.

"Let me tell you one thing ... when Mr. Evil comes through that door, you stand on your feet and pay him the respect that I demand and deserve," hollered Mr. Evil, referring to himself in the third-person. "You see that belt right there. I have earned your respect. So, I expect everyone out here to stand, or I'm going to come out there and slap you upside the head."

It appeared that the three-hundred-pound Mr. Evil was the embodiment of Satan himself—that was until he removed his trench coat, revealing his large belly, which in my view lessened his previously threatening stature.

While Mr. Evil warmed up, Rob Adonis, with a towel around his neck, made a grand entrance, high-fiving little kids before mounting the top rope to greet the cheering fans.

The bell rang, and with a quick drop kick and a flip, Mr. Evil landed his girthy ass right on top of Adonis. The crowd went wild. Things got much worse for Adonis as Dr. Evil slammed him to the mat, strangling him with a towel, and crucifying him with a guillotine.

"That's illegal ref! That's illegal!" screamed the chubby redheaded kid.

Adding insult to injury, the champ handcuffed Adonis to the ropes and then let his manager stomp on, choke, and kick him.

To a sea of boos, Mr. Evil raised his arms in the air, signaling retention of the Ultimate Christian Wrestling heavyweight belt. Poor Rob Adonis was left handcuffed in the ring.

"Hold on, we got a little more," announced Dr. Shock as a few tired fans began to head towards the exit.

Rob Adonis, free from the ropes but with one side of the handcuffs still locked around his wrist, had something symbolic to say. "As I'm looking at this chain wrapped around my wrist, handcuffed, as I was handcuffed to this rope, I'm reminded of a message I want to share with you," he told the crowd. "This represents the chains of bondage within a person's soul. Are you living a life right now that's got you shackled in chains? There's only one addiction out there, and that's the addiction to Christ!"

Clearly moved, the wrestling crowd was once again on their feet, hooting and applauding with their fists raised in the air.

"Woo!"

"That's right!"

"Amen bro!'

To conclude the evening's festivities, the pastor of Harvest Church entered the ring with one final sales pitch. "God brought wrestling to our area!" he proclaimed. "If you want to make that decision tonight to follow our lord Jesus Christ, stand up."

As a line of small children were led by trained counselors to a small room for more prayer, Adonis boasted about the UCW's grand tally of saved souls. "Tonight, we topped over three hundred souls saved!" he exclaimed. "Eight to ten people made a move tonight!"

With the bone-crunching, soul-saving spectacle complete, Dr. Shock summarized the impact of UCW's mission: "Everywhere we go, it's gotten bigger and better. And it's because of Jesus. Put him first, and you ain't got a problem. So, as far as wrestling goes, it's Christian wrestling or no wrestling at all."

# LIVE FOR FREE OR DIE HARD

## TRIBES
Freegans
Squatters

## TRIBAL LEADERS
Freegan Mike
Steve from Homes Not Jails

## WHERE TO SPOT TRIBE MEMBERS
Digging Through Grocery Store Dumpsters
Breaking into/Living in Vacant Buildings

## TRIBAL TRAITS
Sticky, Orange Hands / Covered in Garbage Juice
Black Stocking Caps / Zipped-up Jackets

# FREEGANS

Right in front of me, bags of trash lined the street. My hands were sticky and covered in garbage juice. A dog approached and peed on one of the food bags I was about to look through. Various degrees of judgment emanated from the faces of nicely dressed passersby: a young couple quickly diverted their eyes, and an older man offered a sincere expression of pity. Unfazed, I returned to my task: rooting through someone else's garbage.

"I'm going to feel around and see if there's any meat that I want," said Freegan Mike as he dipped his arm deep into a garbage bag and pulled out from the bottom a handful of gooey muck.

"This is lasagna," he informed me. It had been on the store's salad bar before being tossed out. "I have no shame. I will take that if I want and put it in a bag." He proceeded to do just that.

Mike and I were on the sidewalk in front of Morton Williams, a specialty grocer on the Upper West Side of New York City, sifting through their garbage bags, which were abundant with buried food: creamed spinach, stuffed cabbage, bruschetta, and ham.

"There's a stigma attached to this," said Mike as he ripped open a garbage bag filled to the brim with two-day-old bagels, which he claimed weren't as good as the ones from Pick-A-Bagel. "I don't know if I can take any because they're not whole grain" he said, expressing his discerning taste.

A block away on the front steps of Church of St. Paul of the Apostles, homeless people were fast asleep, presumably unaware that a feast of gourmet food awaited them within the nightly discards left on the curbside. But according to Mike, even though this abundance of food exists outside of every grocery store in Manhattan, a sense of misguided pride prevents most homeless people from taking part in *freeganing*. In fact, the attached stigma and misguided pride turns off the majority of all people from the freegan lifestyle, but Mike doesn't mind.

"If a ton of people did this, there wouldn't be that much food at all," he said. "But the vast majority of people wouldn't even consider it—or haven't thought of it."

As we continued to sift through the garbage in front of Morton Williams, Mike spotted a friend entering the store. "Going shopping?" he asked the man. "We're freeganing. Are you jealous?"

As part of a growing movement that attempts to reclaim needlessly thrown out food, Mike identifies as a "freegan." But freeganism is nothing new; proponents have been dumpster diving since the at least the 1990s.

Mike's type of gourmet dumpster diving—call it "yuppie freeganism" (if you will)—has become more popular among the middle-class. Independent of the obvious political, environmental, and social reasons, the movement has attracted Americans who simply want to save money. Mike's motives, however, are apolitical. He isn't anti-consumer, nor is he poor or living an alternative lifestyle as a gutter punk who frequents Burning Man. He makes good money and lives in a nice part of Manhattan.

In cities such as New York, where it is expensive to live, regular people, including Mike, engage in freeganism as a form of extreme personal finance: it allows them to save enough money so that they can splurge on other necessities or vanity purchases.

"Fifty percent of all food is wasted," he explained. "Some of it is consumer wasted. Most of it is thrown out to make room for the next shipment. So, you get tons of packaged foods."

To emphasize his point, Mike held up a sealed package of expensive (seven dollars per pound) ham that was covered in fruit rinds. "Ninety percent fat free," he read from under the pulp.

Mike first discovered freeganing in 1994. While walking home from work, he stumbled across a café that had thrown out perfectly good sandwiches. So, he took the sandwiches and passed most of them out to the homeless, saving a few of the discarded consumables for himself. Today, Mike estimates that eighty percent of his food comes from freeganing. But he won't eat just anything out of a trash can. He only wants the gourmet stuff.

"Between the fancy sandwich emporium and the supermarkets, you can find everything from high- to low-end stuff being thrown out," he told me. "You can get dairy. You can get meat. You can get gourmet food. This one place across from my gym sometimes has sushi." I cringed at the thought of "dumpster sushi."

Some people, by reselling what they find, actually make money off of the things they discover in dumpsters. But that isn't Mike's goal. He simply tries to find only organic, high-end food that he can eat, and if he can find it in the trash bags right in front of an upscale grocery store, then so what.

Since stores throw away food when it's expired, when it's bruised, or when a new shipment arrives, some of the food found in dumpsters is still cold. As a result, Mike often recovers high-quality meats, cheeses, and other perishable items for free that earlier in the day would have commanded a premium from a typical shopper.

Most stores toss the trash around nine o'clock at night. "You got a narrow window. If it's out too long, the garbage men will take it," Mike said. "Sunday nights are good because supermarkets usually don't throw out goods over the weekends."

It also helps Mike to know the exact type of food that each place pitches. Morton Williams, for example, is the best store to score fruit, dairy, and food items discarded from the salad bar, which means rummaging is going to be messy. So, it's important for him to bring something with which he can clean his hands.

The proper freeganing essentials are plastic bags for the food, water to wash hands and dirtied food, and paper towels. Clothes should be something that one doesn't mind getting caked in garbage. Before going through the bags, Mike advises freegans to feel the outside in order to get an idea of what's inside. And a basic freegan ethic is to open up the garbage where it ties and seal it back up when done. "You don't want to slit it like it were the belly of an animal," he explained.

Mike, who is a health-conscious weightlifter and tries to eat only the whole-grain, high-protein foods he finds, has earned some strange glances while picking through the trash. "People see a middle-aged white guy doing this and you can see their shock. You can see fear and loathing and disgust," he said. "Unlike people who have to go through garbage to survive, I have this option."

Sometimes, passersby assume that Mike is, in fact, homeless and offer him money or food, but he disarms them with a friendly, "Hello," and instructs them to extend their kindness to someone who is in need. "People are curious, but they also have a kind of revulsion," he said. "But when people listen, they tend to understand."

Our last stop was Gristedes, arguably the most expensive grocery store in New York. The garbage bags looked as if they were someone's gourmet shopping bags. "Even though there are rats out, they'll scurry if you're nearby," Mike advised me.

We dug through the Gristedes garbage and pulled out unspoiled treasure after treasure: cold sesame noodles, eight cartons of cheddar jalapeño spread, linguine, eggplant tortellini, and mangoes. "Sometimes, if I'm hungry, I'll eat a little here and there and then put it in the bag," Mike said with a melon in one hand while scooping out the fruit with the cupped fingers of his other hand. By that point of the evening, my hands were orange and sticky, and I realized that I smelled like a salad bar.

After finishing the melon, Mike found a party veggie tray and held it up. "I don't want this, but it's nice." He decided to take it and give it to his neighbors. He also grabbed a fancy cake to give to his building superintendent.

At the end of the night, Mike had ten bags full of food, more than he could carry. Spread out on the sidewalk, our plundering had yielded several hundred of dollars' worth of food that was all sealed in packages, under their expiration dates, and still edible.

"Sometimes I hate to get anything else because it's too much to carry," he said as he lugged his food sacks down Ninth Avenue to the roar of cabs rushing by. "But if I don't eat it, it will just go in the garbage."

Although the food is gourmet, most people still get squeamish when Mike tells them where it came from. "The vast amount of people won't do it because they have conditioned disgust about it," he said. Yet Freegan Mike's building superintendent didn't mind the fancy cakes, and his friends have never complained about eating the reclaimed bruschetta, ham, creamed spinach, and beef stir-fry.

"Even though this is more for my personal benefit, it's still something that is good for the environment," he said. And screw what most everyone else thinks. After all, it's perfectly good food.

# SQUATTERS

**M**Y NEW SUBLETTER FORWARDED me a copy of a letter—demanding the actual monthly rent I paid for my apartment—that she previously had sent to my landlord. The letter began: "I am a senior executive professional in the world of technology … I indicated to Mr. Leon that if he cannot provide this information, then I would find other means by which to exercise my right."

The wheels were turning—wheels that would eventually cause me to lose my one-bedroom, rent-controlled San Francisco apartment. My subletter—a senior executive professional in the world of technology—had moved to San Francisco less than a year earlier. She was holding my apartment hostage with the goal of blackmailing me into paying her money and then grabbing the place for herself.

When it comes to the sense of entitlement associated with San Francisco housing, it's a cutthroat world.

As a result of the tech industry takeover, art-related jobs in San Francisco had dried up, and I needed to go where work was available. So, I took a job in New York that was going to last for a few months. My plan was to put an ad on craigslist and sublet my apartment. I knew that if I gave up my rent-controlled apartment, I would never again be able to afford to live in San Francisco. (My only option for decent living would be across the Bay in a nearby neighborhood known as "Oakland.")

Plus, San Francisco was full. According to a 2016 report by the U.S. Department of Housing and Urban Development (HUD), the rental market in the greater San Francisco area had an estimated overall vacancy rate of 3.1 percent, down from 5.2 percent in 2010. My fully-furnished, rent-controlled apartment was being sublet for $2075 per month—a third of the current market price. In fact, the rent was almost $1400 below the current asking price of an average one-bedroom San Francisco apartment, which—according to data collected by *Curbed* in September 2017—was around $3,400.

My subtenant, therefore, was getting a sweet deal. The few hundred extra bucks per month I made on the place went to moving and travel expenses, not to mention the additional high-maintenance pain of subletting to a newly transplanted "senior executive professional in the world of technology" ... or anyone for that matter. The previous time I rented my apartment, the subletter destroyed the walls by drilling holes into the closet doorframes in order to add a lock to keep her "very expensive jewelry" safe.

This nefarious housing climate has turned San Francisco into the Wild West and the have-nots into Third World citizens who rent out their homes to rich Westerners as if they were living in Iron Curtain-era Prague. But instead of greeting the affluent at the train station and showing them apartment photos from a leather binder, we simply list our places on Airbnb or craigslist and send an Uber to pick up our wealthy strangers at the airport.

It's a new class system. We're not supposed to sublet our apartments, but we do so anyway in order to make ends meet. Besides, who—other than perverts—wants a stranger they found on the Internet masturbating in their bed, even if it's to earn money?

Economic Darwinism in San Francisco has driven out anyone who makes less than eighty thousand dollars per year. For example, a San Francisco office temp earning fifteen dollars per hour—which equates to $2600 a month before taxes—is relegated to a life with roommates. And if evicted by their landlord, they suddenly could find themselves in a dire situation.

The newly-arrived techies—with their Google bus sense of self-entitlement—have driven up rents to outrageous sums and currently plague a city that was once mythologized by the freaky-people of counter-culture. Now, the freaks that remain are left screaming into the midday sun, looking for new options and grasping at what was taken from them long ago. The San Francisco housing crisis has bred a vicious ecosystem that's motivated by greed, animosity, and survival.

In San Francisco, people want apartments—no matter what it takes.

In dark contrast to the methodology of a newly arrived "senior executive professional in the world of technology" who poaches a rent-controlled apartment, Homes Not Jails takes action by breaking in to vacant buildings. Formed in 1992, this activist faction believes housing is an inalienable right and seeks out unoccupied spaces for homeless people to inhabit. As long as people are forced to live on the streets, these anarchists have vowed to open squats in unused structures.

In this gentrified economy, it's hard enough for San Francisco artists, but what about those who are just seeking a roof over their heads? Since a big part of the ethos of San Francisco was spawned out of the Summer of Love and helping those less fortunate, I decided it necessary to tag along with a group so passionate about keeping San Francisco diverse that they would do it by any means necessary.

"Monday and Tuesday nights are ideal times to look for places. People usually go to bed early," stated Steve, who sported a modified Mohawk and SF Seals jacket, as we walked along the silent streets of the Mission district. "The best time is after 11 p.m."

Steve and Brian (not their real names) comprised the evening's away team (an idiom taken from *Star Trek*). First, we made a pit stop at their headquarters in the basement of a tenant's rights building.

Brian's unemployment benefits were about to run out, and he was looking for housing options in the priced-out renters' market. Within the cramped quarters, labeled boxes were filled with all the provisions—crowbars, lock cutters, dead bolts, screwdrivers, tape, nails, lock picks, sleeping bags, car batteries for electricity, and flashlights—needed by a squatter to secure a San Francisco property.

"It's the worst squatting in all the country," Steve said of San Francisco. "But it can be done!"

When an average two-bedroom apartment rents for $4,400 per month (and three-bedrooms can go for over $5,000), building owners are very protective of their properties. While it's risky to occupy a building owned by someone else, police—due to liability issues—can't take direct action to remove squatters until a property owner signs a form granting them authority. The legal consequences for violators are minimal: police process them, issue a misdemeanor citation ("suspicion" of trespassing), and let them go. Rather than bothering with the lengthy hassles of the legal process, building owners often encourage squatters to leave on their own accord by making them cash offers.

Potential San Francisco squat locations can be found online at HUD's website (hud.gov), which provides a list of foreclosed homes, and on the city department's blighted list that trumpets vacant properties deemed in need of repair.

"It doesn't mean the place is viable. But that's a start," Steve explained. "You should look for who owns the property. Are their taxes paid up? Do they have any liens? The best leads are to get addresses of places you see on your daily routine."

We put on black stocking caps and zipped up our jackets. Steve grabbed a backpack full of equipment, and the away team headed out. With sheets of paper in hand, we steered through the heart of the Mission to check out a street-level unit that was scouted the night before.

"Those lights weren't on last night," noted Steve. "Go with a couple of different kinds of tapes or wire and secure any type of entrance.

A produce-tie wrapped around a door or gate is very effective. See if it's broken when checking back to determine if someone has been inside."

Before entering a place, there are a few other things to look for: a lockbox, which is not really a lockbox but a box that has keys inside; a For Sale sign or any notice of a public hearing; and the presence of trash cans on garbage day, since a vacant place doesn't need to put out garbage.

Once inside, it's important to look for an alternative route in which the premises can be entered on a daily basis. Satellite maps, such as Google Earth, can help determine if the property has an alley or a backyard. Then, after securing the place, it should be made to look like a home, as if the squatter is legally there. Good squatters have mail sent to the address, set up the PG&E bill in their names, and keep the place clean.

"Scout it out to see if it's truly vacant," Steve said. "Look through the windows and shine a flashlight through a mail slot. You don't want to get inside and hear someone snoring. It's the worst feeling in the world."

I nervously nodded my head in agreement.

At the next locale, fortune took another ill-fated spin. "The chain on the gate wasn't there last night," Steve remarked. Although a piece of tape still indicated that the front door had been untouched, the newly affixed chain was enough of a deterrent to halt pursuit of the premises any further.

Under California law, a person who lives on a property for more than thirty days is considered a "tenant." So, a landlord can't just kick them out.

In a sense, my subletter was squatting in my apartment, but I really had no legal recourse to evict her. Technically, any Airbnb guest could turn someone's apartment into a squat (a lot of blind trust is put in the sharing economy system). Booting out a squatter from an Airbnb or craigslist rental could be a long, difficult, and costly process. San Francisco tenant attorney Joseph Tobener was quoted as saying that he gets fifteen calls a week about Airbnb properties. The calls fall into four categories:

1. Landlords evicting tenants to rent units through Airbnb;
2. Tenants complaining about neighbors using Airbnb;
3. Tenants being evicted for subletting through Airbnb; and
4. Airbnb hosts who can't get guests to leave.

With one month left in her sublease agreement, the "senior executive professional in the world of technology" was angered when I told her that I was moving back to San Francisco and it wouldn't be possible for her to stay two additional months beyond our stated agreement. But, unfortunately, she was ready to take action to ensure that she could stay even longer, thereby leaving me with no place to live.

Contrast her position with Steve's vastly different ideology on San Francisco housing. "Even if you can be there for a night or two, it's much better than sleeping on the streets," he said. "It could be a place for twenty-three hours a day, or it might be a situation where you have to be out by seven every morning. That could work out for someone with a job they have to go to."

As if my apartment were a hostage and the "senior executive professional in the world of technology" its kidnapper, my subletter had demands: "If you don't furnish the information requested, a statement of your monthly rent as well as a statement including the costs of my energy consumption, I will pursue other ways of securing it." This letter brought me undue anxiety. A San Francisco landlord will use any possible reason to evict a tenant, who—for the previous ten years—had been living in a rent-controlled apartment. Why? In order to make room for some millionaire willing to pay quadruple the rent because they just created an app that allows people to draw funny mustaches on cat photos.

Between 2009 and 2015, the number of yearly no-fault evictions in San Francisco soared from 544 to 1352—a one hundred forty-eight percent increase. An annual report issued by the Eviction Defense Collaborative highlighted some of the outrageous reasons greedy landlords use to evict tenants. Violations cited by property owners included offenses such as "parking outside the parking lines" and "cooking during nighttime hours."

Under the Ellis Act, if a San Francisco landlord wants a tenant to leave in order to jack up the rent, they are required to pay the tenant between $5,555.21 and $16,665.59. But under one of the law's many questionable loopholes, I could have been evicted without receiving a payout: just a thirty-day notice to vacate the premises along with the forfeiture of my deposit. As a result, the Ellis Act is now a friend of money-hungry landlords.

The thirty-one-year-old law has been used to evict ailing seniors and those with disabilities—some who have been living in their rent-controlled apartments for decades. The tenants of entire buildings have been evicted, and senior citizens have died while fighting their Ellis Act evictions.

As the San Francisco real estate market skyrocketed, Ellis Act evictions spiked to an all-time yearly high of 349 in 2013—a one hundred fifty-five percent increase over 2009 levels. Since 1994, there have been over seven thousand Ellis Act evictions.

Steve is very familiar with the foibles of the Ellis Act. He knows of greedy landlords who would rather keep a low-rent building completely vacant for years and then maximize profits when rental prices skyrocket

While navigating our course, we passed several homeless people sleeping in corridors. Steve pointed out a forty-six-unit SRO that had been vacant since 1991. Apparently, the owner refused to sell the property to groups wanting to turn it into low-income housing. In 2010, Homes Not Jails staged a public occupation of the building to demonstrate the availability of vacant housing for the homeless.

Finally, we approached our last location: an eight-unit apartment building that had been vacant for at least five years. Steve already had been inside the building, and that night, he planned on securing the place for squatters.

"At least I want to get my rope back I left on the roof," he said with a smile.

Huddling together like those people you see on the streets that seem to be up to something, we made a plan.

"You post up here," Steve said, positioning me across the street.

Then, Steve turned to Brian. "I want you to hold your bike, so I can climb up the side of the building and grab onto the fire escape," he instructed. "If there's any danger, or you see someone paying too much attention, I want you to text me."

The duo strolled far down the block—bike in hand—and then crossed the street. After a small trickle of drunken people passed, Brian held his bike steady, and Steve, Spider-Man-style, quickly scaled the side of the building, heading towards the roof and disappearing out of sight.

I watched the vacant building until three in the morning, with no sign of Steve stirring inside. Finally, Brian received a text: Steve had secured the building for squatting. A door opened, and a look of reassurance washed over Brian's face. He had a place to live when his unemployment benefits ran out.

My story, however, did not have a happy ending. I lost my rent-controlled one-bedroom San Francisco apartment and never moved back.

The "senior executive professional in the world of technology" wrote to the SF Housing Board: "Mr. Leon, he denied me my rights and has illegally been taking advantage of the rising rents in SF and exploiting the newcomers that he so ironically scorns as having a sense of self-entitlement. Mr. Leon is the one who has been exploiting the landlord."

Then, she submitted an application to take over my apartment. But once she learned that her new rent would be three hundred percent more than what she was paying me to sublet, she moved from my old place into a far less desirable neighborhood (not Oakland). Apparently, this tech professional felt bad for the landlord, who she thought was not making enough money.

Ultimately, we both lost; only the landlord won. After I moved out, he raised the rent higher than a motherfuckin' Google-launched Internet balloon. This type of unbridled greed has fueled the vile San

Francisco housing ecosystem, where low-income people are forced to leave the city or resort to breaking into the vacant buildings that line the Twitter-paved streets of gold.

Yes, I had been exploiting the sacred institution created by San Francisco landlords, who patiently waited for old people to die. But unlike them, I was unsuccessful.

Now gutted of its character by tech invaders, San Francisco is a very different place. I no longer recognize the city, an unknown metropolis where new residents feel bad for property owners: the same wealthy real estate robber barons that we used to call "the man."

I'll never move back to San Francisco, but I often think about Brian and hope that he has a roof over his head.

# SILLY, SILLY WHITE FOLKS

## TRIBES
Fans of Jerry Springer
Tanning Addicts
White Supremacists

## TRIBAL LEADERS
Jerry Springer
Anti-science Tanning Industry Executives
Kevin the Racist

## WHERE TO SPOT TRIBE MEMBERS
In the Studio Audience at *The Jerry Springer Show*
Tanning Salons / Dermatologists Offices
Neighborhood Restaurants

## TRIBAL TRAITS
Enthusiastically Yelling, "Jerry! Jerry! Jerry!"
White People with Unnaturally Golden-brown Skin
Casually Dining and Reading Hate Literature

# FANS OF JERRY SPRINGER

IT STARTED OUT INNOCENTLY enough. I contacted the publicists of *The Jerry Springer Show* and told them that I wanted to write a story about the process the show employs to book its rambunctious guests. My plan was to spend a day behind the scenes as a fly on the wall, observing the show's guest bookers as they wrangled the guests and convinced them to expose their most shameful secrets on national television.

"The producers are very protective about their guest bookers and guests," I was told by the show's publicist. "The producers have decided to pass. I wish I had better news."

I wondered why the producers were so protective of the methodology the show used to select its guests and then exploit their most vile qualities in front of a live studio audience notorious for shouting: "JER-RY! JER-RY! JER-RY!"

The task proved much easier than I had ever imagined. As it turned out, all I needed was a burner phone, a concocted story, and some actor friends.

I went to the *Be a Guest* page on the show's website and responded to every single guest scenario that they requested. Using the pseudonym Armando Leoni and a series of different email addresses, I fabricated numerous stories, touching on all *The Jerry Springer Show* hotspots: cross-dressing, cheating, gay sex, meth, drama, incest, etc.

Two days later, I received a voicemail: "We are actually booking for this week's show. If you're interested in coming on, definitely call me back." The show had responded to the following scenario: "Are you gay or transsexual? Is your partner always trying to meet people on Grindr and you want them to stop?"

With plot points written out on notecards, I returned the call.

"*The Jerry Springer Show*," answered the perky-sounding guest booker. "Are you looking to be on the show?"

Responding as if I were an erratic, upset man whose world was crumbling, I asked, "Should I explain the situation?"

The woman replied, "Just the real situation, not the situation for the show … whatever your real situation is."

I was not sure what the guest booker meant. Did potential guests usually have two different situations: a real one and a made up one to use on the show? Since I had neither, I weaved a tale of debauchery, claiming that I was a gay man whose partner, Tony, was addicted to engaging in anonymous sex via Grindr … AND IT WAS TEARING US APART!!!

"You basically want him to stop the bullshit and be focused on you," she said, paraphrasing my words. "Do you think he would want to go on the show with you?"

Already somewhat disturbed by the fact that I was being coaxed into revealing intimate details about my fictitious life, I asked, "So how would I go and approach him in doing that? I don't want him to freak out."

Her advice: "You can tell him whatever you want to get him on the show. You can be up front with him and say, 'I got a call from *Jerry Springer*, and they want us to come on the show.' And you can be like, 'I don't know what it's going to be about' and just see what he says."

I then added a plot point as to why we urgently required *The Jerry Springer Show* to save our relationship. "I really need to confront

Tony because I have a medical problem. I have a rare blood disease. That's why it's important for me to make this work out," I said, clearly implying that my time left on this planet was very short.

"Really!?" she excitedly interjected. "Oh wow!" I could tell that the wheels in her head were turning. "We could do a hypothetical situation. Do you guys have another gay friend that we could say Tony hooked up with? So we could bring out a friend—that's down to play along with it—and say he hooked up with Tony."

I was confused. She wanted us to fabricate a scenario, which was something I was already doing without her help. In an attempt to get my fake story on the air, the guest booker seemed to be acting as an additional partner in crime, thus bringing my concocted story to a new level of fiction.

"I know in real life you want to confront him about Grindr, but I don't know how we can make that work for a show if we don't have anyone we can bring that's talking to him on Grindr," she informed. "You know what I mean?"

After pausing for a moment to try to comprehend her words, I replied, "Yeah, okay. I understand."

Next, she brainstormed the following scenario: "So, for the show, we could say, 'Armando is here, and he's suspicious that his boyfriend, Tony, has been messing around with him behind his back.' Then, Tony comes out and says, 'I have to tell you something. I hooked up with a friend, blah blah blah.'"

The guest booker was good—even better than me—at creating bullshit stories. "Okay, yeah. I think I get it."

But she was not finished. "Or we could go a different way. Just see if Tony wants to come on the show," she persisted. "We'll figure out a story after that."

Even more confused than before, I again questioned her: "So does it have to be someone that Tony has hooked up with?"

She replied, "No, it doesn't have to be. It just has to be someone that would feel comfortable to say that he did. We can fabricate it for the show. "

*The Jerry Springer Show*'s guest booker had just offered to further fabricate my already fabricated story. Her dishonesty was throwing my dishonesty for a loop.

"Okay, um, yeah. That's fine," I said.

"I don't know what your schedule is like, but we have a slot open for this Tuesday to be on the show," she stated, offering an all-expenses paid trip to New York. "You'd come out Monday, do the show on Tuesday, and be back Tuesday night."

The guest booker then called my friend Tony DuShane, who I had recruited to play the role of "Tony Knox," a Grindr enthusiast.

"I think you guys would be super cute to come be on the show," she said.

With a backstory that involved cheating on a significant other by hooking up on Grindr, why in the hell did she think that we would be "super cute"?

Explaining on the phone to Tony that it was necessary to concoct a storyline, the guest booker said, "Basically, we would have to add another person to your story, because it's *The Jerry Springer Show*. It's like drama. If you have another friend, we could do a cheating story or something, and we can just exaggerate the drama you have. Do you know what I mean?"

Tony replied, "Oh, yeah. Okay, okay," before adding a double-plot-twist—meat for the Springer audience—to his concocted Grindr grinder story. "What if Armando doesn't know that some of the sex was unprotected?" he said, mentioning that his anonymous hookups usually occurred during drunken, meth-fueled blackouts.

"Ha! Ha! Ha!" laughed the guest booker at the new plot twist. "I totally get it. All right, cool."

To those employed by *The Jerry Springer Show*, unprotected and drunken anonymous gay sex while on meth was, apparently, funny.

"You guys sound really cute, and I would love to work with you guys," she cheerfully said to Tony. "We could do any kind of story. I'm thinking like your story will be you've been hooking up with other people, and you bring on someone you hooked up with. We could find a friend that could play that role—of someone you hooked up with."

The guest booker then indicated that she was excited at the prospect of a gay couple fighting on the show. All she seemed to want was a story that contained ridiculous conflict, and it didn't matter if a donkey showed up, just as long as fireworks went off.

"Yeah, that makes a lot of sense," said Tony.

"So, do you know someone who would want to come on with you guys—someone that knows your relationship and could say you guys hooked up?" she asked.

"Oh, okay. Yeah, yeah, I have a couple of people in mind, but I'll ask them first because I don't want them to be surprised," Tony replied.

"Call some friends and ask them if they want to come on *The Jerry Springer Show* with you. We can definitely make the story work," she suggested. "We could have you as the cheater in the relationship, and then bring a guy friend that's down and cool to say, 'Yeah, I hooked up with him.' You're there to show you really want to be with Armando, and we'll make it a happy ending."

Basically, *The Jerry Springer Show* was no different than the WWE, where, in an orchestrated script, good struggles versus evil in order to get the audience frothing at the mouth. It seemed that the show had no intention of helping guests; for the price of a free trip to New York, they simply wanted to exploit people's fucked up human problems.

An hour after Tony spoke with the guest book, I called her. Sounding panicked, I expressed worry that my relationship was beginning to unravel. "I think Tony might have spoken to you," I said. "He sent me this text, and it was hard to understand if he was angry or not angry."

She confirmed the conversation with Tony: "Yeah, I talked to him. He said he's going to look for a guy friend who could come with you guys and be part of the story."

Acting extremely grateful, as if I thought she were doing some great good for humanity, I replied, "I thank you in advance. Going on the show would really help resolve our situation and improve our relationship."

The booker tried to put me at ease. "He was like, 'This will prove to him that we have a real relationship ... and this will shut his family up too,'" she said, laughing.

I lined up my buddy Brad Kuehnemuth, who previously had helped me infiltrate *Judge Joe Brown* with a fabricated case, to play Tony's fictitious Grindr fuckmate: "Big Daddy Dino." Just to be clear, Brad was playing a guy who was pretending to be a guy who was pretending to be a different guy.

"These fucking freaks want me to come down and do the show?" said Brad in character to *The Jerry Springer Show* guest booker during his screening phone call. "I think they want their asses beat on TV. They want Big Daddy Dino to come down and teach them a lesson."

Ecstatic, the guest booker explained the scenario to Brad. "They need a guy who can say they hooked up with Tony for the show. Does that sound like something you could do?" she asked.

"Yeah, if I'm allowed to smack them around on TV, for sure," replied Brad, aka Big Daddy Dino.

The guest booker loved Big Daddy Dino. "I'm definitely going to give you a call tomorrow and give you more details," she said. "And I'll set up a story with the three of you!"

Surprisingly, neither Tony, Armando, nor Big Daddy Dino received the promised return phone call from *The Jerry Springer Show*. So, I called the guest booker, and she informed me that we had been bumped to the following week. "Our next available show would be Sunday and Monday of next week. I don't know if you guys would be available for that week?" she asked.

"I just have to know a little ahead of time because it's hard to get off of work," I replied.

"I'll be back in the office on Thursday," she said. "So, I can definitely let you know then."

When Thursday rolled around and *The Jerry Springer Show* had not called, I phoned the guest booker and left her a voicemail. Tony and Big Daddy Dino did the same.

A few hours later, I called her again: no answer. That time, I left a panicked message: "I'm wondering if you've spoken to Tony because we got in an argument, and he hasn't talked to me since last Sunday. Can you please give me a call back?"

She never did. We were blown off by *The Jerry Springer Show*, discarded with yesterday's dysfunctional news and thrown to the wayside. Perhaps she had found a more fucked up Grindr addict whose troubles made our concocted story in comparison seem too tame.

Sure, I was only trying to infiltrate *The Jerry Springer Show*, but what if I really had been a meth addict looking to the show for help, putting my blind trust in a guest booker who promised a happy resolution? My hope would have been stirred up while my life remained trapped in emotional hell. No wonder the producers were so protective of the sleazy shenanigans employed by the overzealous guest bookers who led the chants of "JER-RY! JER-RY! JER-RY!

# TANNING ADDICTS

I FELT DIRTY AND ethically bankrupt as I sat shirtless on an examination table inside a dermatologist's office. Around my wrist was a hidden-camera-equipped watch. With my chin resting on my hand, I tried to look casual as possible while pointing at moles on my body and asking the doctor if she thought they were cancerous. The hope was to capture on my hidden camera a "gotcha" moment, where the doctor would say that my moles weren't cancerous but for insurance purposes report them as such.

But there was no gotcha moment. "If you want to get things removed for cosmetic reasons, I don't know if your insurance will balk at that," said the dermatologist, who only supplied me with a gift bag of samples of skin moisturizers and sunscreens.

I had been hired as a shill for the tanning industry. At the time, I was broke and needed work. So, I put on the hidden-camera-watch and went undercover into dermatologists' offices, attempting to document that these medical professionals, as my employers believed, were only concerned with profit when warning the general public about the dangers of tanning. The men who hired me thought that the footage I obtained would be used by *60 Minutes* as part of a grand exposé on how medical science was trying to squash the poor, misunderstood indoor tanning industry, which had earned a bad reputation due to the fact that over excessive tanning causes cancer.

To make matters worse, the World Health Organization had classified tanning beds as "carcinogenic to humans." As a result, the tanning industry decided it necessary to enter into public relations mode and spin the "facts" in their favor. While on the offensive, they attempted to discredit critics: dermatologists and the American Cancer Society.

According to the tanning industry's conspiracy theory, dermatologists benefited financially by frightening people into their offices for skin cancer checks, and the American Cancer Society benefited through increased donations. By implementing sketchy marketing tactics, the tanning industry sought to demonstrate that medical professionals operated only for sinister purposes, including trying to shut down their business. Furthermore, they wrongfully claimed that medical professionals were killing more people than big tobacco by attempting to cut off a key source of vitamin D: tanning beds.

Due to my previous infiltration work, I was recruited and hired to go undercover with a hidden camera into dermatologists' offices and expose the grand mal sun scare conspiracy. It was my job to unclothe a corrupt system bent on ruining everyone's bronzed beach party and crushing the innocent five billion dollar tanning industry. My undercover adventures were referred to as "sting operations." In reality, I felt as if I had completely sold out all my journalistic integrity for a paycheck.

On our initial phone call, the tanning industry guys told me that they were convinced that my findings would evoke multiple news segments and debunk the "evil doctors" who were more concerned with lining their pocketbooks than protecting the safety of the pale, untanned public. My infiltrations were to show that profit, not health issues, was the entire motivation behind the sun scare.

To aid my quest, I was provided with a briefing sheet entitled "Undercover Sting," which posed numerous questions designed to combat actual scientific evidence: in the U.S., each year, tanning beds account for as many as four hundred thousand cases of skin cancer, including six thousand cases of melanoma, the deadliest form. According to the National Cancer Institute, melanoma has risen by one-third in women under forty—the target demographic of tanning salons—since the early 1990s. This evidence led the FDA to classify tanning beds as potentially harmful medical devices, its most serious risk warning, which resulted in forty-one states restricting tanning salon use by minors.

But reality didn't matter to the men who hired me. Their "Undercover Sting" sheet provided me with all the "data" and questions I needed, including this gem: "The US has four and a half percent of the world's population, yet, if you compare the American Cancer Society's melanoma estimates to those of the World Health Organization, we have forty-seven percent of the world's melanomas. How can you explain this?"

Along with the "Sting" sheet, I was provided with several articles about a handful of dermatologists who, over the years, had been convicted of fraudulently collecting insurance dollars after intentionally misdiagnosing patients with skin cancer. The tanning guys wanted me to make it appear as if this illegal behavior were the industry norm. How was I to do this? By documenting that when harmless moles were removed, doctors were paid insurance money and false skin cancer data were added to the melanoma statistics.

"Start by finding several moles that are obviously not skin cancer and that you would want removed for strictly cosmetic reasons. You want to make it clear that you know this isn't skin cancer, and you want the doctor to confirm that it isn't as well," they instructed me. "We want to prove that this is blatant fraud by removing what is known by all parties to be a benign mole and billing the insurance company as a skin cancer."

Following an examination, per the instructions, I was supposed to try to talk the doctor into turning in the procedure to my insurance as a "precancerous lesion" or some form of skin cancer, thus proving that dermatologists were part of a rogue, money-making network that risked their credibility by making fraudulent claims to insurance companies and, therefore, falsely increasing the incidents of melanoma in the United States. It was supposed to be the gotcha moment.

So, playing along with my new employer's game, I made, against my better judgment, appointments at several dermatologist offices and loosely followed the script: "Hi, Dr. X. I have this mole that I wanted to have checked out. I've been reading a lot about melanoma recently, and I'd really like to get this removed."

But it turned out that every single dermatologist I encountered followed ethical guidelines. "I'm sorry, but your insurance doesn't cover it. You could go to some derm offices that would lie and say that it's irritated. I can't do that," stated the first doctor I visited. "It's something I don't want to do—start lying on charts. They might do that for you. But I just like to do things how they are done."

Furthermore, my undercover journey started freaking me out after I visited the second doctor, who asked me if anyone else in my family had been diagnosed with skin cancer. Instead of exposing a charlatan skin cancer money laundering ring, I was starting to worry that my moles were actually going to be diagnosed as dangerous and cancerous.

"Yes, my dad," I said, noting that he recently had skin cancer surgery. "Should I be worried?"

The doctor replied, "Just be responsible. If you know you're going to go to the beach for two hours, then use sunblock. If you're working in the office all day long, there's no reason to use sunblock."

When one dermatologist pointed out that the exposed veins on my nose were a direct result of damage from excessive sun exposure without sunscreen, I actually got into the habit of applying sunscreen in my daily life.

With my doctor's office infiltrations proving unsuccessful, the tanning guys had one final task for me: pose as a reporter and call the mother of a young woman who died from melanoma caused by excessive indoor tanning. I was to tell the grieving woman, an outspoken advocate against the tanning industry, that I wanted to write a story about her daughter's life. They wanted me to use tabloid tactics to force the woman to admit that her deceased daughter's skin cancer condition started long before she became addicted to indoor tanning.

I felt like vomiting … or crying, especially after reading what the mother wrote about her daughter: "My precious baby girl was my best friend, my hero, and the light of my life. I will do everything I can to continue her fight against melanoma because I know that is what she would have wanted. I miss you, Sweetie Pea, and love you with all my heart."

I never again spoke to the tanning guys. Like with all conspiracy theory purveyors, they spun facts and scientific data to suit their agenda. According to these guys, indoor tanning was only deemed harmful to increase profits for dermatologists; sunscreen was only recommended to line the coffers of sunscreen companies. It was utter nonsense.

Still, despite the known dangers, some people—in an attempt to achieve the tanned, Barbie doll standard—ignore the surgeon general's recommendation and continue to brown their bodies in tanning beds as if they were chickens in a rotisserie oven.

But I know better. My work, therefore, was not in vain. From now on, it's sunscreen, sunscreen, and more sunscreen. By becoming a shill for the tanning industry, it turns out that I unknowingly became a shill for both dermatologists and the cosmetics industry, thus proving the existence of their master plan. Gotcha!

# WHITE SUPREMACISTS

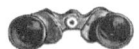

IT WAS A TYPICAL Friday night at a neighborhood restaurant in Davis, California. Clean-cut couples, carefree college students, and happy families with small children dined as perky servers bounced from one table to another. I was purposely forty minutes late to my dinner meeting with three white supremacists that were for some reason under the impression that I was an eager new recruit.

I had met the white supremacists while trolling the Internet for hate groups and decided to infiltrate this group in order to find out exactly why they were so filled with hate.

Using the pseudonym Hal Haterman, I sent them an inquiry email after rejecting various other hate groups: the Aryan Nations, the World Church of the Creator, the National Socialist Movement, the White Aryan Resistance, the White Power Liberation Front, and, of course, the Ku Klux Klan. To protect my own safety, I've chosen not to reveal the name of the hate group, but trust me, it's a good one! The organization claimed to be a direct spin-off of the old American Nazi Party, which sees itself as carrying on Hitler's dream to purify the white race and prevent Jews and African Americans from degrading "our" culture. Its website railed about "the Negroid filth churned out by rap music and the other Jewish promoters of anti-white music intended to demoralize, corrupt, and deracinate young whites."

While waiting over a week for a reply, I became rather paranoid. Not only am I a member of a religion that they want to wipe off the planet, I also had the uneasy feeling that the FBI added me to a watch list.

"We should have our next meeting coming up mid-to-late January," stated the local leader of the hate group in his reply. "I would like to meet with you in person before then."

As any normal person should be, I was a little bit freaked out, but against my better sense of reason, I messaged back, "That sounds great! Where shall we meet?"

He responded, "How about Applebee's? I'll be coming with my wife, baby, and one other member."

I had a date with hate! And who doesn't love Applebee's?

As I drove the one and a half hours from San Francisco to Davis, I nervously became sick to my stomach. My reason for choosing to arrive late: I wanted the white supremacists to hate me.

I approached the perky Applebee's host and explained to her that I was supposed to meet a guy named Kevin, his wife, a baby, and another member of their group. "They promote our culture, you know," I said with a wink.

"Right this way," she answered with a bubbly smile, not computing my hidden meaning. The host led me past tables of joyful families and right to the three white supremacists—and a baby. They were already eating appetizers and had frowns on their faces, apparently upset at my lack of punctuality. Despite the scowls, I was taken aback by how "normal" they looked—just like everyone else at Applebee's. The guy had short hair and wore a plain button-down shirt, and his wife looked like a typical soccer mom with baby in tow. The third racist was a dumpy, blond college girl, hardly what I expected.

"Glad to see that you made it," said an unsmiling Kevin, who works in computer software.

"There's nothing I hate more than traffic. Except, of course, the Jews," I said, apologizing to the haters, still dumbfounded and disturbed at the normality of the situation. Surprisingly (or not surprisingly), they agreed.

Initially, nervousness abounded as they tried to feel me out while also attempting to impress me with the merits of their hate group. I, meanwhile, pondered whether my fork would work as a weapon—in case I needed to defend myself.

"Can we get a menu?" asked the white supremacist soccer mom to the bubbly Applebee's sever.

"What made you want to get involved?" Kevin asked.

"It's either complain or do something. It's better to do something than complain," I said, throwing verbiage from their website right back at them. They seemed pleased.

After some arbitrary racist small talk about Mexicans, Kevin, without fanfare, placed some *White Identity* hate literature on the table.

"This tells a little bit about our organization, our ideology," Kevin explained. "We also have our application on the back, if you decide to sign up."

The application asked prospective members to attest to the following: "I am a White person of good moral character, with no ineligibility. I want to build a secure and healthy future for my race by becoming a member."

Before I could read any more, Kevin placed a magazine on the table. "It's kind of like *Time*," he said, "except it's for us."

Fortunately, our overly cheerful server approached with the food. "Okay, who had the salad?" she asked.

Kevin quickly covered up the hate literature with his forearm before asking me where I lived. I informed him that I was thinking about to moving from the Bay area to Davis.

"It's really horrible about the Asian problem there," proclaimed the dumpy blond college girl, chiming in with her first blatantly racist comment of the evening.

"Uh, yeah … the Asian problem … that's why I'm planning on moving up here," I reluctantly replied, trying not to blow my cover.

"It's probably a lot better up here. At least you won't have to see a lot of Asians," she spewed with a vicious, hate-filled laugh.

"So where would you suggest moving?" I asked.

"You're not safe anywhere," announced Kevin.

The table grew silent. I fiddled with the straw in my water glass, not knowing what to say. Finally, Kevin piped in as he placed on the table what appeared to be an indie magazine geared towards hipsters. "This is our music magazine," he said.

"Oh yeah? What kind of music do you write about?" I asked, well aware that the group's website described exactly what type of music white supremacists were supposed to prefer: "polkas or waltzes, reels or jigs" but not "negroid jazz or rock rhythms."

Kevin boasted, "All kinds of music."

"Yeah? Well, your website said the kind of music you guys are into is polkas," I noted, trying to rain on his hate-filled music parade. "It said not to listen to rock and roll and instead listen to polkas."

He seemed mildly embarrassed. "Uh, sometimes we have the wrong people working on the websites," he professed, attempting to save face.

"I have an article in this month's new issue—about my experiences going to school at UC Santa Cruz," proclaimed the dumpy, blonde college girl. "It was pretty much a liberal freak show. But it totally transformed me. I went there not really knowing anything. It changed my perspective for the better. It made me a much better person."

By "better person," she apparently meant "racist-to-krazy-Ku-Klux-Klan-zealot."

At UC Santa Cruz, she was shocked by the emergence of her roommate's "wigger traits," which included partaking in atrocities such as singing black music and inviting black friends into the dorm room. In an act of rebellion against human decency, the dumpy, blonde college girl decorated the dorm room with iron crosses and Nazi swastikas.

"How is everything?" asked the bubbly Applebee's server, who seemingly had popped out of nowhere.

"Can I get some nachos please? They look delicious," I said, wanting to see if white supremacists hated ethnic food with the same passion they hated ethnic people. For good measure, I also ordered an Oriental Chicken Rollup, which is in and of itself casually racist.

"So what goes on at a meeting? Do we organize protests? Have bake sales?" I asked.

"We're going to be doing some big flyering this weekend—race flyers," Kevin explained. "I know the media is going to jump all over that."

The leafleting was to be done in what they called drive-bys, where the flyers, like newspapers, were launched out of car windows onto residential driveways.

"We try to put out a positive message—that people can go out and promote their own race," Kevin said.

My Applebee's nachos finally arrived, and let me tell you, they were absolutely delicious.

"So, how many members do you have?" I asked Kevin.

"I don't have the exact figure, but we are the largest racial-activist organization of its kind in the country," he said. "It could be a couple thousand. We have a good size unit here. Each meeting we have thirty to forty people."

According to Kevin's wife, most of the members are in their late twenties to early thirties. "There's a lot of couples with kids. We're very family-orientated," she said. "In our unit, there's about fourteen kids, total. At the meetings, there will be little kids running around everywhere. Yeah, we're really family-orientated."

Kevin added that their group was a great place for professional networking. "We have all kinds of members," he said. "Doctors, lawyers, professors."

Typically, the meetings were held at various restaurants or the public library, but the next meeting was to be held at, believe it or not, the back room of a German restaurant. Claiming to be an amateur videographer, I asked Kevin if I could film the meeting for posting on their website.

"That wouldn't be a good idea," he said. "Like if we're planning a certain event and the opposition sees it, they might plan a protest. We want to be as open as possible, but there's also people out there who hate us. And they want to do anything possible to destroy us."

While adjusting my hidden audio recorder, I replied, "That's a good idea. You guys shouldn't tell your secrets to anyone outside the group you can't trust. They could spread the secrets."

It was time for dessert. The perky Applebee's server described the options.

"We want to get one of those sweets with the brownies and the chocolate and the ice cream," said Kevin's wife to the smiling server.

I knew that members of hate groups loved ice cream!

"Do you guys do things, like have get-togethers with other groups—like the Klan?" I inquired.

"We tried it in the past, but it just didn't work out," Kevin solemnly admitted. "It wasn't our ideology; it was more personal conflicts. Some members had a little too much to drink and started arguing. We like to present the best representation of the white race that we can."

Kevin knew a little bit about the Klan. He did a two-year stint with the Klan in Texas but wasn't happy about the experience.

"The Grand Wizard was on welfare," he recalled. "He was about fifty years old and lived with his mother. It was really depressing. We had to go with him to get his welfare check."

In a moment of contrived honesty, I puffed out my chest and stated with an air of cockiness, "You know, I've been kind of looking around at a lot of other white racialist groups. I'm still deciding which one to join. The Church of the World Creator doesn't look that bad."

All three white supremacists at my Applebee's table collectively rolled their eyes. I had struck a nerve. Apparently, hate groups even hated other hate groups.

"I think overall our organization has a higher level of intelligence," said the dumpy, blonde college girl. "I don't want to sound snotty, but it's true. I think we attract the best of the best."

Kevin then explained what separates his hate group from others.

"At our meetings, we make sure everyone wears a shirt and tie. We make sure of that. We want to represent our race in the best possible manner," he said. "We want to change people's impression of what a white racialist is. We're all not evil people. We're all not sickos and weirdos."

As other patrons at Applebee's sat laughing and enjoying their meals, I wanted to escape and get the hell home. But before I could, Kevin asked one final question: "What religion were you raised?"

Caught off guard, I inadvertently announced that I was Jewish. Their faces turned whiter than a Klansman's sheet. "Just kidding," I stated as the table breathed a sigh of relief and let out a nervous laugh.

As we headed towards the door, fearful that I might be ambushed by other members hiding outside in the bushes, I said, "I'm going to go back and use the bathroom, but it was really nice meeting you."

Kevin, now making full eye-contact with me, said, "Well, wait! Nancy's going to go to her truck and get you some stickers to hand out."

I tried to spend as much time as possible in the men's room, hoping that the white supremacists would be gone when I exited. But there they were with a stack of crude, homemade stickers that read: *Earth's Most Endangered Species: THE WHITE RACE. Help preserve it.*

Before leaving, I had one last question for Kevin: "What made you decide to join the organization?"

He paused and then turned a bit reflective. "I always hated minorities," Kevin bluntly stated. "I've always never really liked being around them. They always made me feel uncomfortable."

While looking for depth and an intellectual explanation behind the ideology of white supremacy, I found nothing. All I discovered were the racist ramblings of a bunch of floppy-shoed clowns who did nothing but put the "ha" in hate. Hate groups hate; it was as simple as that.

# COMEDY TO
THE RESCUE

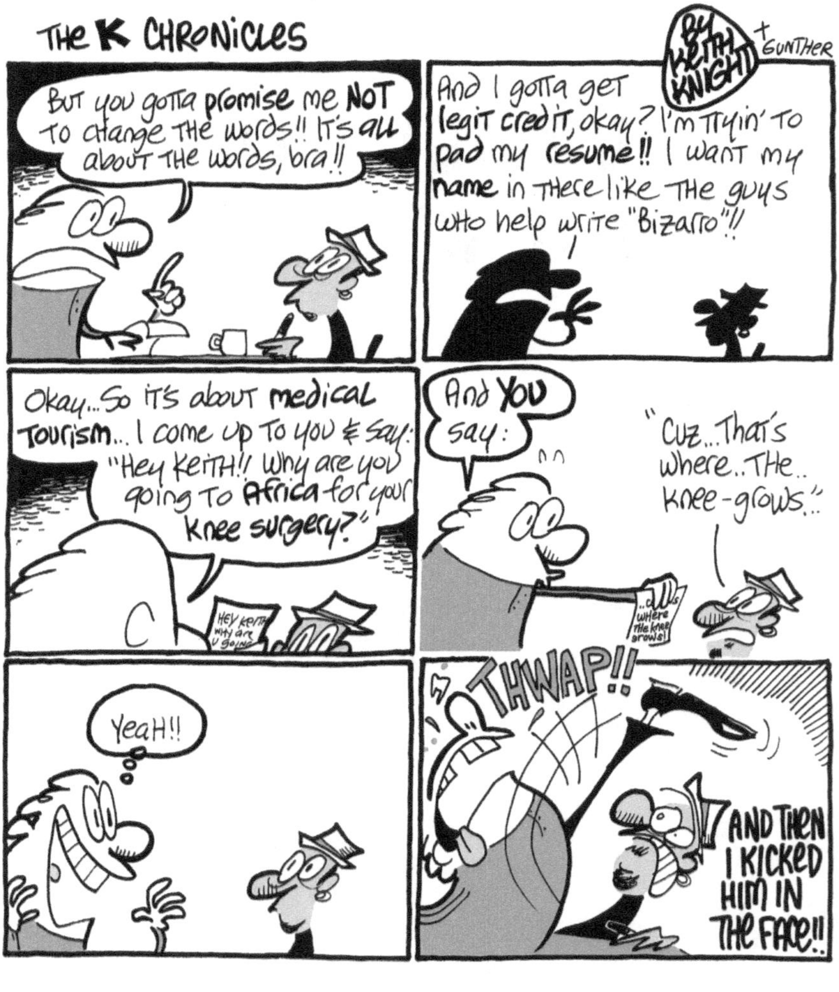

## TRIBES
Presidential Joke Writers
Cuban Comics
Christian Comics
Fans of "The Juice"

## TRIBAL LEADERS
Bruce Cherry / Mark Katz / David Litt
Ricardo Isidron / George Smilovici
Chonda Pierce / Nazareth
OJ Simpson

## WHERE TO SPOT TRIBE MEMBERS
The West Wing
Teatro America / The Streets of Havana
A Christian Church Near You
The Same Room as "The Juice"

## TRIBAL TRAITS
Pacing the Old Executive Office / Wearing Out Shoes
Using Humor to Distract from Suffering
Telling Jesus-centered Jokes
Running to (or from) OJ Simpson

# PRESIDENTIAL JOKE WRITERS

**B**RUCE CHERRY IS ADAMANT that George W. Bush is one of our greatest, naturally gifted comedians—well, at least amongst former U.S. Presidents. A staunch liberal, Cherry professed to me: "Bush is perfect for comedy. He knew how to pause and deliver a line. He's actually good. He's just a natural."

And Cherry should know: he reached across the aisle and wrote comedy material for Bush to deliver at many prestigious events, including the White House Correspondents' Association dinner and the Alfalfa Club—an annual gathering of the most powerful political movers in Washington.

In politics, jokes serve as a powerful means to humanize politicians, connect with an audience, and influence people. And when used strategically within a speech, humor can translate into votes. Cherry can count himself a member of those select brethren of writers who—by penning jokes—have made our commanders-in-chief appear wittier than Oscar Wilde.

"Everyone wants to be able to tell jokes. And if someone can't be funny, we think less of them," said Cherry. "If someone can be funny, it's impressive. You think that person can think on their feet. It's a skill."

Cherry's presidential-joke-scribing-proclivities were discovered by a famous mom. After writing for Comedy Central and Air America, he landed a gig with a speech writing company called Head Writers. One of their clients, Steve Bridges, was a successful George W. Bush impersonator.

"Barbara Bush saw Steve at an event and loved him so much that she told George," Cherry recalled.

Bush and Bush's doppelgänger soon appeared together on stage at the 2006 White House correspondence dinner. Cherry, along with a team of writers, penned the material for the Bush duo.

"The funny thing about writing for George Bush, conservative audiences loved dumb George Bush jokes," Cherry said. "George Bush loved them!"

Brother Jeb, at an Alfalfa Club dinner, actually delivered the favorite Bush joke Cherry ever wrote: "George told me he's thinking of running again. I said, 'George, the Constitution prohibits you from running for a third term.' He said, 'Wow, they put my name in the Constitution!'"

But some of Cherry's liberal friends weren't so keen with his new choice of employer. "There are people I know who would unfriend me if they knew I've written for Bush," he declared.

So, Cherry thought to himself that there was nothing wrong with taking the Bush job: "He is the President of the United States, and I am an American. So fuck it. I'm definitely not going to turn that down, even though I disagree with everything he did. It's not like I'm moving his Iraq plan forward. I'm just letting him tell a few jokes."

But Cherry does have standards. He turned down comedy writing gigs for both Rick Santorum and Mitt Romney. "The amount of money was insane," he said. "I thought about it and was like, 'What if I take this job and Romney wins?' I'll have the biggest payday in my life, but it would cost many people their health insurance ... including me."

Mark Katz was the point man responsible for injecting humor into Bill Clinton's speeches during his eight years in the White House. "People used to complain to me, 'You mean the president doesn't even write his own jokes?'" Katz said. "I'd look at them and say, 'Tell me the number of hours a day you want your president writing jokes? Just give me a number, please ...'" His comeback quickly shut down that line of complaints.

"What I liked most about writing for politicians was pushing out the parameters of what they were able to say in public," Katz said. "Being part of the best strain of our political dialogue, where politicians are telling more truths [and] saying the things using humor that they would otherwise strenuously deny the other three hundred sixty-four days of the year."

During his first meeting with Clinton, the president was unclear on the importance of self-deprecatory humor in his political speeches.

"He could not understand—for the life of him—why he would stand up and tell jokes at his own expense," Katz recalled. "It made zero sense to him. He looked at me like I was crazy."

Fresh out of college, Katz shared an office with a young George Stephanopoulos during the ill-fated Michael Dukakis presidential campaign of 1988. From there, he wormed his way into the Clinton White House, one presidential joke at a time.

"Jokes is actually the wrong idea," said Katz, regarding his approach. "It's really about what's the idea for the speech. What does the speech need to be? And then comes the jokes. Jokes are an execution, but the speech needs to be ideas."

When constructing presidential speeches, Katz, who now runs the Soundbite Institute (a creative think-tank), employed a strategy that used humor to convey something that was not easy to say.

"You're talking to the joke writer who helped the president navigate humorously through impeachment," Katz stated. "The only [other] person to do that was Andrew Johnson's joke writer—and he kept very poor notes. So, I was on my own."

Additionally, President Clinton's first one hundred days in office were a rocky affair. Katz's witticism modus operandi for Clinton utilized self-directed humor. Take this joke about another unfortunate president that he penned for Clinton: "I don't think I'm doing that bad. After his first one hundred days in office, William Henry Harrison had already been dead for twenty-two days."

You see, Clinton solved his problems by using humor. Once he conceded the obvious, then he could buy back credibility. And credibility is valuable political capital.

"Humor flatters where spin insults. It's a signifier of intellectual honesty," said Katz. "If this person is being honest with himself, then I trust this person to be honest with me ... Humor is: 'I think you're smart enough to understand what it is I'm trying to say here.'"

Invariably, Katz would ask a politician to remove a joke from a speech if they were not completely sold on it. "I know if they don't believe in it, it's not going to work," he said. "Until you believe in a joke, you really should not say a joke out loud."

During his entire writing stint for Clinton, Katz—while walking the parameters of the old executive office and mumbling to himself, "What's the idea?"—wore out ten pairs of shoes.

"It's kind of a mind-meld. You're lending your sensibilities to someone greater than yourself—in this case, the president. I would stare at a blank screen and say, 'If I were this guy, what the fuck would I say?'" Katz recalled. "Eventually, you arrive at the idea for the speech, and then you start writing the jokes and execute the idea in a funny way."

After preparing a draft, Katz would have dozens of meetings with Clinton, who would then select the material that he thought worked best.

Shoes aside, the real challenge Katz encountered while writing humor for the president was trying to get the jokes approved by the staffers who could nix them. "In the White House, there are maybe ten people who can write a joke, and there are two hundred fifty people who can kill a joke," he said. "So, you're trying to get a speech through that gauntlet. That's the real challenge."

For David Litt, President Obama's former speechwriter and lead joke writer for numerous White House Correspondents' Association dinners, things worked a bit differently. "Because I was writing regular speeches most of the time, [I had] a general sense of here's what's crossing a line—in a bad way—and here's what's pushing the envelope—in a good way," Litt said. "I wouldn't say we sat around and thought about rules. And I certainly never set down a document saying here's the dos and don'ts for the people pitching jokes."

Before finalizing what made the cut for Obama's White House Correspondents' Association dinner monologue, Litt would write roughly six hundred jokes. "The president would read [the jokes that made the final cut] when he read the rest of the speech," said Litt. "Obviously, if someone thought it was inappropriate, they would say so, and we'd talk it out and decide whether to keep it in. And ultimately it would be up to POTUS to make that call."

According to Katz, it took Obama a while to find his true comedic voice. "He's got the charisma of one hundred men. You can't teach that," he said. "And that's a God-given skill and talent. So, the speech in his hand becomes his own, and he delivers it as only he could."

Cherry believes that President Obama has great—and natural—comedic timing: "He pauses anyway, and that works really well if you're doing dry humor, which is the stuff they give him. It's very thoughtful and works out perfectly to the way he talks."

So what about Donald Trump?

"What's interesting is, President Trump has a sense of humor," said Litt. "It's a very classic bully's sense of humor, in the sense of the kid giving another kid a wedgie on the playground. It's doing something that's amusing and entertaining to onlookers, but it's not necessarily a well-crafted joke. It's using humor as a constant way of asserting status. So humor becomes this tool to remind people that you're the dominate one in the room."

Unlike the comedy protocol for Obama, Litt doesn't feel that Trump has political advisor Stephen Miller leading a team of joke writers for speeches. Largely, he says, it feels as if Trump is mostly ad-libbing off the top of his head.

"Does it look written down to you? I don't think so," said Litt. "Look at his rallies—he gets laughs from the audience. I don't think anyone is writing those jokes. Then again, the laugh tends to be about punishing enemies rather than about making friends, if that makes sense. Some people say, 'Isn't that insult comedy?' Not really. When you're a politician, it's just kind of being a dick."

Katz feels that humor isn't a part of Trump's shtick: "Trump has thrown out the entire political playbook as it existed before 2016. Nothing that he does corresponds to the standard operational procedure of using humor to win and influence people."

Trump's interpretation of humor, according to Katz, fails in all aspects of the standard, effective political paradigm. "There's nothing kind. There's nothing self-defacing. There's nothing self-directed. There's nothing honest," he said. "[Trump's jokes] exist to hurt. So humor is probably the wrong word for it."

Cherry added, "[Trump's] not funny. He's just mean. That's what sells him. People who want mean like him."

Is Trump's problem simply that he has bad joke writers?

"I promise you, there were jokes that would have suited him a lot better—[jokes] that he crossed out," Katz said, recanting what the writers of Trump's 2011 Comedy Central Roast went through. Penning jokes for Trump was an arduous task for the comedy writers for the roast. Unlike Bill Clinton, they found that Trump was incapable of self-deprecation and lacked the ability to laugh at himself. The writers found themselves in a battle with Trump about whether or not they could make jokes about his hair. Topics the powers at Trump Tower also deemed off-limits were Trump's past bankruptcies and any suggestion that Trump was not as wealthy as he boasted to be.

"I'm sure [most of the jokes] were left in the trash can of history," said Katz. "The speaker is the ultimate filter, and he makes the speech his own with the choices he makes."

Katz doesn't even think he could have salvaged Trump's roast speech. "I would have gotten no further than anyone else would have gotten," he said. "Eventually I would have been escorted out of the room by security. I don't doubt it was in the grasp of any human to give him the help he needed."

Litt agrees. "I'm sure Donald Trump is not an easy person to write speeches for," he said. "But I don't think you can separate it. I mean, if you write jokes for a celebrity—and they're hard to work with—you can sort of separate the act of writing from the person you're writing for. I just don't think that's possible when it's the president.

"I think for a president, telling jokes, it's not the most important thing they do politically. But the reason presidents try to be funny: it helps them convince the American people that they're doing a good job, that they have the right set of values and priorities."

# CUBAN COMICS

**F**OR NEARLY TWENTY YEARS, Ricardo Isidron, the godfather of Cuban comedy, has been producing *La Esquina de Mariconchi*, a live comedy showcase that features some of the island nation's hottest talent. When asked by my translator if Cuban comedians were allowed to do jokes about either the deceased Fidel or his brother Raul, he uncomfortably replied, "No! No! No!"

To Isidron, even mentioning Castro jokes during a casual interview in the back of a theater felt risky. "In their private lives, Cubans do jokes about Castro ... but not in public," said Isidron. "The comedians just have to work out a strategy to tell jokes without mentioning names."

For example, a comedian might refer to Fidel as "The Beard," a code word understood by nearly everyone in Havana. Or a comedian could play off the fact that Fidel was born in August by presenting a scathing horoscope about Leos.

In a country where freedom of speech is not guaranteed, this type of creativity is necessary. Satire becomes even more relevant, especially when the powers that be are trying to stamp it out. Just as Cubans, for decades, have dealt with shortages of food and other general goods, the island's comedians must be resourceful and use their ingenuity when making political jokes. It often creates hilarious comedic tension.

"A comedian on stage could yell, 'Down with Fidel!' said Isidron. "And then, after a few beats, 'Martinez!'"

Over forty years ago, Isidron began his career as a comic but was forced from the stage when he developed throat problems. As a writer and producer, Isidron has become one of the country's most instrumental figures in the contemporary stand-up scene. In fact, he is probably the foremost expert on Cuban comedy, which often roots its humor in the culture's economic suffering at the hands of the Castros and the U.S. embargo.

"There's a hotel. It's got these two beautiful swimming pools," shared Isidron. "One's small and one's big. The manager says, 'Look what beautiful pools.' The guest goes, 'Yeah they're beautiful, but they're empty.' The manager replies, 'No, we got no water, but they're beautiful pools.' The guest says, 'Yeah, but they're empty. So what do you do?' The manager replies, 'We fill them with dirt, and we grow trees.'"

Isidron and I both laughed.

"This is what happens here in this country," he added. "It's absurd."

Cuba's comedy history dates back to the nineteenth century, when Spanish theatre troupes performed in Havana. During the Batista regime, American organized crime turned Havana into the Las Vegas of the Caribbean, where U.S. comics, such as Jerry Lewis, regularly performed at the casinos.

After the Revolution, which ended in 1959, the tenor of Cuban comedy drastically shifted. Shortly after Castro seized power, Leopoldo Fernández, a comedian on the hugely popular satirical radio show *La Tremenda Corte*, was blackballed after performing a political comedy sketch as his beloved character, Potato. The bit employed classic, Cuban misdirection. A fellow player pulled out a photo of Castro; Potato went to the wall and said, "Allow me. I want to hang this one myself …"

According to Isidron, the modern era of Cuban stand-up comedy started in 1991. One of the first breakout stars, Álvarez Guedes, performed deadpan one-liners: "A guy meets one of his friends on the street and says, 'Do you like women with tits?' His friend replies, 'No, just two.'" (The pun, which is lost in translation, is supposed to imply that the friend believes the man to be talking about a woman with more than two breasts.)

Censorship has prevented Cuban comedians from having access to American stand-up comedy. As a result, their comedic influences have come from their own comedy history and other Spanish-speaking countries. For example, Dominican comedian Julio Sabala, who specializes in musical impressions, such as Julio Iglesias and José Feliciano, has influenced the modern Havana scene.

Currently, Panfilo is Cuba's most famous comedian, thanks to the hilarious and warm-hearted videos he created with Barack Obama during the former president's historic trip to Cuba in 2016. Isidron told me that the viral videos were censored from YouTube in Cuba mere days after being posted.

For the most part, Cuban comedy is respectful of American presidents, and there isn't too much Trump comedy being performed. "There are a lot of comedians doing impressions," said Isidron. "And in their impressions, that's where they express their opinions."

George Smilovici walked down his Havana street as if he were the mayor of the block, stopping to kiss women on the cheek and saying '*hola*' to people he passed.

"Here, I feel like I'm at home," said Smilovici, who was born in Cuba to Jewish immigrants from Romania. He performs comedy in Australia for half the year and spends the other half in Havana, where he also records original Cuban compositions with his orchestra, Frente Caliente.

"Here, they respect the balls of a comedian, just to be up there," Smilovici said of Cuban audiences. "It's because of the freedom angle. Politically, there are certain things you can't talk about. On stage, they expect the truth. And they respect anybody that goes out there and talks the truth. That's what comedy is all about—bursting bubbles."

According to Smilovici, selling your heart before trying to sell the material is the key to winning over a Cuban audience. "They have to love you and feel the warmth," he said. "If someone gives, they will get back ten times more. If you engender love and compassion, then you got them in the palm of your hand."

Smilovici told me that Cuban comedy is family oriented and more innocent than comedy elsewhere. "Here, they don't like swearing," he said. "They're very timid and conservative in some ways." Instead of using crude slang for a man's privates, a comedian will opt for the word "*pinga*," which literally translates as "stick."

Conversely, there is no political correctness in Cuban comedy. "Here, they make fun of everything," remarked Smilovici. His jokes, which he claims are done without malice, range from body-shaming bits about the way people look to off-color observations about race and sexual orientation.

While Havana resonates with vibrant colors, lively music, and warm people, its struggles with poverty are apparent to any visitor. "People take their own toilet paper on the street here," said Smilovici. "Because when you go into a public toilet, like at a bar or restaurant, they don't have toilet paper."

In Cuba, doctors only make around sixty pesos per month and often need a second job to provide for their families. Comics, however, can earn much more, approximately twenty paseos per show. Local comedy clubs pay a percentage of their earnings to the government-controlled union, and the union then pays the comics.

"In a country that suffers a lot, where you have so many problems and people are under so much stress, you have to have humor," said Smilovici. "Humor is not a luxury, like in Australia. The poor suffer more. The poor need more jokes."

On the night I visited, it was *La Esquina de Mariconchi's* eight hundred forty-seventh show. The sold-out crowd of all ages filed into Teatro America, a beautiful sixteen hundred seat art deco theater.

As the lights dimmed, the red curtain went up, revealing

Mariconchi, the host, who was wearing a wig and a woman's dress. "There's a guy backstage who said he wanted to take a boat to Florida, but it was very bad weather, so he couldn't go," quipped Mariconchi to big laughs.

An audience member playfully heckled him, and Mariconchi offered a sharp comeback: "Be quiet … or else you'll end up being a prostitute on the street!"

Three women, there to celebrate birthdays, were brought on stage. Mariconchi forced them to compete in a lip-sync contest and awarded the winner a prize of toothpaste, which was considered a good prize as a result of the frequent toothpaste shortages in Cuba.

Most of the comedy on display would appear old-fashioned to U.S. comedy fans. Enoel Oquendo, who looked like a pudgy version of Larry Wilmore, told straight-up joke-jokes accompanied by a musical sting and a little dance move after each punchline. He concluded his set with a long joke that involved the simulated humping of someone from behind. Holy pinga!

Duo Espatula—a classic comedy double act featuring a tall, skinny guy and a short, chubby guy—was pure joy. The duo began with an ironic statement about the current Cuban economic situation: "Can we have a minute of silence. Let's remember the seventies, eighties, and nineties—all the years when we had everything. And now we have nothing."

The comedy pair then broke into a song with the chorus: "Everything was great before, and now it's shit. Obama can't take anymore away from me!"

A warm, cathartic laughter echoed throughout the theatre. Everyone present knew what it was like to lack the ordinary necessities that much of the world takes for granted.

"There's only one way to look at life in Cuba, and that's through humor," whispered Smilovici. "If you look at it the other way, it's really sad. There's only one option: you have to laugh. Life here is hard, but there's an incredible love inside."

# CHRISTIAN COMICS

I WAS ON STAGE at His Hands Church in Cobb County, Georgia, delivering a bunch of Jesus jokes I wrote on a napkin in my hotel room the night before. It was going well.

"I used to play in a Christian punk band. We were called the No Sex Before Marriage Pistols." Big laughs emanated from the crowd. That joke was preceded by: "My brother was given a name right from the Bible. My parents named him 'Locust.'"

As one of the winners of a Christian stand-up comedy competition, I earned a slot performing in a show at the annual conference of the Christian Comedy Association (CCA). It was a big accomplishment for a dreadlocked, Brooklyn Jew who had gone undercover posing as a Christian comic.

On paper, pretty much every comedic obstacle was working against me, such as having to deliver religiously oriented, squeaky clean material. But the crowd at His Hands Church gave applause breaks to several of my jokes, including this one: "I have an atheist friend. The only problem is ... I don't believe he exists."

At one of the comedy workshops, we were told that a stand-up routine is like a one-act play. Except in this one-act play, I was portraying a guy very similar to myself—only he was a homeschooled Christian comedian. Yes, I had entered the world of Christian stand-up comedy, where setups, callbacks, and punch lines were used merely as devices to spread the word of the Lord. (**Spoiler Alert:** I don't find Jesus in the end.)

The first thing I noticed at Christian stand-up comedy gatherings was how damn nice everyone acted. Even comedians who looked at me as if I were an axe murderer acted nice.

Roughly one hundred Christian comedians from around the country gathered inside His Hands Church for the two-day conference, which included panels, prayers, networking, and performances—all aimed at serving God through stand-up comedy.

"All the jokes, all the workshops, all the meetings are nothing without the Lord by your side," said CCA's president Kenn Kington, who kicked off the comedy conference. "Let us follow you, Jesus."

A Bible passage from Corinthians appeared on a large screen, and the comedians bowed their heads in a prayer geared towards their profession: "Father, thank you for the way you gifted us ... It's only through the gift of Jesus that we do this for you."

In this alternative comedy universe, Christian stand-up comedians starred in their own holy stratosphere with routines that employed the same ingredients as traditional stand-up comedy. Virtually unknown to the mainstream comedy world, some of these comics have had multi-platinum records.

"I perform wherever I can," said a newbie comedian—and dead ringer for Shaggy from *Scooby Doo*—who traveled from California to attend the conference.

"Do you do mainstream clubs?" I asked as we congregated near the food table.

"Yes, but I have to plug my ears," he said, regarding the foibles of being a Christian comic in the land of two-drink minimums and blue material. "Everyone is just trying to be dirty for the sake of being dirty. Even Chris Rock says you have to start out clean."

He had a point. The night before I arrived at CCA, I attended a hipster comedy show in Atlanta, where a bearded guy did a bit about his cat lapping up fresh cum following sex with his partner.

There wasn't even a joke attached.

On the other hand, the Jesus-centered Christian comedy was squeaky-clean and was often tied to an inspirational message. Needless to say, there were no dick jokes. From what I saw at the conference, the comedy was mostly comprised of observational humor about things Christians do, such as going to church or doing household chores for their wives. "Our entire purpose is so we can be around others who are doing this and see why God gave us this crazy gift," explained Kenn. "And that really is what this is."

Within the Christian comedy circuit, that crazy gift means good money. Headliners reap between fifteen hundred and twenty-five hundred dollars per church comedy show, which amounts to a good living when you consider that there are more churches than comedy clubs. Since a limited pool of comedians exists, and each House of the Lord has hours of programming to fill, comics can quickly move up the ranks.

"Almost every year, there's somebody here that came just to learn about comedy and try to get bookings in churches because clubs are drying up," said CCA Chaplain Gordon Douglas, who also frequently cited scriptures related to comedy. "If you're doing this Christian comedy out of the love of God and because he called you to it, you will know his joy and peace."

I'm not sure I knew what he meant, but I nodded in agreement as the funny pastor asked a magician to come on stage and do a magic ball trick.

"We do no different in the church world than what every evangelist has done since I was a kid," said Chonda Pierce, one of the biggest stars in Christian stand-up comedy, as she addressed the conference. "They have a funny story at the very start. They're trying to capture the audience's attention so they can set them up and deliver their sermon. So, that's what I do."

Pierce, who started her career as a Minnie Pearl impersonator, is now represented by the same manager as Billy Crystal. But due to this niche circuit, she's still unknown in Hollywood. "I got an award this year as the most gold and platinum awarded female comic in history—in any genre," she recalled.

The award presenter leaned over to her and said, "I've never heard of ya!"

It surprised no one. For the past twenty-five years, Pierce has been selling out shows in towns with names like Sedalia, Zionsville, and Silsbee. "In the Christian comedy world, as far as the church goes, being a woman is a plus," she said. "To get a bunch of guys to come out and hear you is pulling teeth for a church. To get a bunch of women to come hear a woman comedian, they'll just come in minivans! My audience has the checkbook; your audience has to have permission to leave the house!"

In the late 1990s, Pierce held the very first CCA conference on her hundred-acre rural Tennessee farm, nicknamed "The Funny Farm." A woman from Los Angeles participated in the gathering and asked Pierce how she could get more comedy work at churches. Pierce replied, "Well, the first thing I'd start doing is wear a bra."

For Pierce, being a Christian comedian means that "at some point in the night, you want your audience to make a decision. That's what Christianity is—we have made a decision to believe Jesus."

She uses stand-up comedy as a spiritual vehicle rather than using Christianity as the purpose behind her comedy. "We all know that nobody is going to buy a ticket if all it says is 'a bunch of people are going to talk about Jesus tonight for twenty-five dollars,'" Pierce said.

Christian comedians seem to be the only group of laugh-slingers that are branded by their faith, possibly because Catholic, Muslim, or Scientologist comedians don't to try to convert their audiences while doing stand-up. Typically, most secular comedians don't have an ulterior agenda other than making people laugh.

"People feel afraid of the title," Pierce said. "It grieves me when I realized later on that it was causing me limitations."

True, the mainstream comedy world doesn't know what to make of Christian stand-up comedians.

I asked secular comedian Brendon Walsh, whose credits include *Late Night with Conan O'Brien* and *Jimmy Kimmel Live*, his take on

Christian comics. "It's the same thing that comes to mind when I hear the term 'Christian Rock,'" he said. "It's like something that this specific group wants, but they can't have the real thing because it doesn't agree with their beliefs.

"It's like being lactose intolerant. You still want ice cream because it's great, but you can't have it because it makes you shit your pants. So they make their own crappy version of it that won't make them shit themselves, but it's just not the same."

Comedian and renowned atheist Doug Stanhope—who has appeared on Comedy Central and in the short-lived *Rosanne* reboot—had a harsher take: "There is no question that religion is born in power and control." He told me that he was troubled by the fact that this ideology spills over into Christian stand-up comedy. "Their followers are guilty of trying to find an easy answer," he said, "whether it's in a book, a sermon, or even a joke, rather than question the quandary of life on their own terms."

This disdainful view of religion by secular comedians can make it difficult for Christian comedians, especially when performing involves sharing a bill with a road comic who likes to party.

It breaks Pierce's heart to see Christian comics compromise their material when they perform at mainstream comedy clubs: "Not only does it grieve me, but I think it also grieves the Father. I think he says, 'Please be the same person that you are.'" Fearless to the faith, Pierce refuses to compromise. "I tell the exact same jokes at the Grand Ole Opry as I do at the First Baptist!"

Diagnosed with clinical depression after the death of her husband and the suicide of a close pastor, Pierce now uses her comedy as ministry to speak to those who might be going through the something similar: "That's what the Lord had designed for me to do."

She sees spirituality as intrinsic to her comedic success. "If you're here because you eat, sleep, and dream your craft, you are going nowhere. You might succeed for a while, but you will eventually crash and burn and have nothing," she said during a comedy workshop at the conference. "Hold your path and deliver the best comedy that you can but don't forget your Father. I can't take you all on and change your career, but I can invite the Holy Spirit into your life and pray for you."

Nazareth—who goes by one name, just like Cher—approaches his comedy with a similar philosophy. "A Christian comedian is someone who wants to honor God every time they go on stage," he explained. "You can be in a prison. You can be in a strip club. It doesn't matter. If you're performing, you want to honor God. Then, God will find a way to honor himself through that."

The CCA chaplain referred to Nazareth as "the James Brown of Christian Comedy" and called him "the hardest working man in the spiritual funny business." Nazareth's favorite joke: "How do you get Holy Water? You boil the Hell out of it."

Born in Kuwait, the bespectacled and energetic comedian started his comedy career in the early 1990s, performing in clubs alongside Chris Rock, Adam Sandler, and Kevin James. Three years into his stand up career, he found his comedy calling: "I gave my life to Christ. I left the clubs and was going to go back to accounting. And God said, 'No, I want you to use this for me.' So I said, 'Can I honor you?' And he said, 'Yes!'"

In 1992, Nazareth fasted for forty days, at which time God allegedly told him to rent a stadium, put on a Christian comedy concert, and start a production company, Comedy Crusades. Now, whether performing at a mainstream comedy club or a corporate event, Nazareth uses the comedy stage as his pulpit to spread the word of Jesus.

"I've headlined the Tempe Improv on a regular night," he said. "I ended up giving an invitation to Christ at the event. Honoring Him allowed me to do it. When you honor God with your comedy, he will use you regardless!"

At the conference, Nazareth led a workshop on acquiring more bookings. Before he began, the comedians bowed their heads and prayed: "Father we do it for you, and we do it for humor …"

For them, praying was not just a ritual. Nazareth said that he has secured more bookings through prayer than anything else. One day, he hopes to perform at the Rose Bowl, alongside other Christian comedians. Until that day arrives, he offered some practical advice to the group: "Say, 'Lord, I'm serious about this comedy. I'm serious about this performing. Can you please open the doors for me? Would you please give me a gig? I need a gig on Sunday.'"

Through this method, Nazareth said that he has picked up last minute bookings, filling in for vacant pastors. "God opens the doors," he claimed.

In the past, Nazareth has also played the "Jesus card"—telling people he's a Christian—as a strategy for scrounging up business. Once, he said, he told the man sitting next to him on an airplane that he was a Christian who performed comedy shows to spread the gospel. "I booked a ten thousand dollar gig on the plane," he added.

But with great comedic powers comes great moral responsibility. "If you're going to be watching pornography or cheating on your wife, don't do comedy at a church," Nazareth stressed. "Say, 'I can't come in today!'"

No matter what a comic's faith, making a living as a comedian isn't easy. It involves the constant need of approval ... and a lot of rejection. In the Christian comedy world, Nazareth's recommended pointers include "stalking your clients."

Cracking the Christian comedy world is all about schmoozing—except it's done with pastors instead of booking agents. Nazareth suggested to *google* all of the churches in a particular area, and then on a Sunday drive to a church, shake hands after the service, and sell them on your comedy. "Tell them this isn't a grocery store," he advised, "where there's one sticker price for Christian comedians."

And when all else fails, Nazareth said to use the power of prayer and God's forces in your favor. For example, if James Dobson, founder of Focus on the Family, is appearing at a nearby church and there's a storm in his home base of Colorado, call the church and say, "If he won't be able to make it, I'm there!" Yet another reason to pray!

"They don't really heckle in churches," said Brian Smith, part of the comedy musical duo Dave and Brian, who have appeared on

*Good Morning America*. Occasionally, someone might shout out, "Rebuke!" But for the most part, church crowds are good.

"Talk about mothers-in-law. Talk about kids," Smith said.

"What about shopping at Home Depot?" I suggested, recalling how on the first night of the conference much of the stand-up material I heard at the showcase involved that hilarious scenario.

Smith added a big, hackneyed Christian comedy standard: "Talk about the differences between white churches and black churches." Sounded, to me, like a bring-down-the-house Christian hacky closer bit.

When it came to lifting material from other comedians, the veteran comic advised, "Though shall not steal. It's right in the Bible."

Next up at the convention was Bone Hampton, who took the stage to provide more advice—and tough-love pointers—to new comedians. Introduced as the "Charles Barkley of Christian Comedy," it was obvious why Bone crushes any room he plays. He has performed at many mainstream clubs and racked up guest appearances on BET, *The View*, and *My Name is Earl*.

Bone, however, had a different attitude than some of his Christian colleagues toward some of the biggest stars in comedy: "This is the hardest thing I struggle with … these L.A. comics. They'll say anything. But there's some stuff you ain't supposed to say!"

Applause erupted, followed by a few shouts of "Amen!"

He continued, "There's some stuff the Lord would tap you on your shoulder and say, 'That's not to be said on the stage I put you on! That's not coming out your mouth to my people!' That's the thing I say about being a Christian comic—don't get caught up with we won't say stuff. We don't do shock; we're not trying to shock people. We do funny!"

Spiritually, Bone just dropped the mic.

Finally, it was time for the Christian comedy competition. Everyone had three minutes to perform their best material. I was nervous as hell before taking the stage. My regular bits wouldn't go over with the Christian crowd. Crossed off was the joke about having a threesome with a pair of Siamese twins attached at the vagina. I had to make these people laugh with clean, well-crafted spiritual jokes. There were just so many variables with which to contend that could make my act go dangerously wrong.

The first comic pointed out that most people abducted by UFOs were usually stupid. His clean, observational humor was as bland as a communion wafer. One woman comic pulled out a pair of electric nose clippers and used the device on herself. A bald guy put on his best (and totally racist and inappropriate) "Ching-Chong-Ding-Dong" voice while doing an impression of a Chinese restaurant chef who cooked cats. Another comic launched into bit about how, when he was sixteen, he couldn't take his nineteen-year-old wife to prom—though he didn't expand at all as to why he got married at sixteen, which might have been a humorous aside to following a theology that prohibits sex before marriage. I wondered if praying would really help these comics get more gigs.

When it came my turn, I simply opted for silly, surreal religious jokes from the notes I had written on the napkin in my hotel room. "I used to be a Mormon comedian," I said. "Here's a joke from my act: 'Take one of my wives, please … because I have several … because I'm a Mormon …'"

When the votes were tallied, by the grace of God, I had sealed a position in the evening's big Christian stand-up comedy show. For a moment, I contemplated feigning a faux demonic meltdown on stage and then closing my set by throwing up pea soup. But after the act before me closed with bit about losing her virginity at an airport, which ruffled some conservative Christian comedy feathers, I decided to play it straight.

In the end, it was me, Jewy McJew from Brooklyn, who stormed the Christian stand-up comedy showcase. Minds were blown. But, more importantly, I had a lot of fun. We were all just stand-up comedians, telling some jokes, messing around on stage, and making people laugh. It was exactly how the world of comedy should operate, where every good set seems like a religious experience. Mine, however, wasn't attached to a magical, invisible sky daddy.

"I've never seen comedy done like that before," a comedian from Des Moines said about my act.

"Do you mostly perform at churches?" asked a comic from Philly.

Then, Bone walked by. "Good job!" he said.

"If Bone likes your act, that's quite a compliment," shared the shunned woman who had closed her set with airport virginity bit.

At that moment, I realized that I was just in a room full of other comedians, all who were from the same island of misfit toys as me. Ultimately, all of us ended up complaining about stuff, dissecting the crowd, and acting slightly jaded. Judging by the number of business cards handed out to me, it seemed as if I could have a career on the Christian comedy circuit. All I would have to do is sign on the dotted line for Jesus.

# FANS OF "THE JUICE"

**I**T WAS MY FIRST big break in Hollywood—my dream had come true. I had been hired to work on a reality television show with an "internationally known celebrity." Actually, I took the job in order to infiltrate the lowest rung of television: a reality show starring an acquitted double-murderer.

On the first day of production, the producer took me aside and dryly explained, "You know, Harmon, we really can't mention ... the murders."

I absorbed the information and vigorously nodded my head. "Okay!" I said with complete enthusiasm. "No mention of murders!"

This simple fact was actually a major consideration when you'd just been hired—off of a craigslist ad, of course—to work on a zany hidden-camera prank show with, of all people, OJ Simpson. You know, OJ, from the slow-speed Bronco chase and the infamous "if [the glove] doesn't fit, you must acquit" murder trial. Yeah, OJ ... as in HOLY FUCKING SHIT, OJ, YOU CAN'T BE FUCKING SERIOUS. That OJ. And I was to be his "funny little sidekick." Yes, the new Kato Kaelin to OJ's ... well, OJ.

In 2005, there was a producer—the same producer who brought the world *Bumfights: Cause for Concern*—who thought it a spanking good idea for the comeback project of an acquitted double-murderer to be a straight-to-DVD, hidden-camera prank show called *Juiced*. The premise was simple. A prank was pulled, and OJ Simpson popped out, exclaiming, "You've been Juiced!" If all went as planned, I hoped that the pranked person would reply, "HEY, AREN'T YOU THAT GUY WHO MURDERED YOUR WIFE AND THAT OTHER GUY?!"

As we waited in a nondescript recording studio in Burbank for the star of the show to arrive, a weird hush fell over the crew when OJ, who was talking loudly on a cell phone, appeared on set surrounded by an entourage of shady-looking handlers. The first thing I noticed about OJ was the size of his head: he had a really large head (in terms of cranial capacity). Immediately, rumors swirled that Warren G, OJ's bodyguard, had just got out of jail and that his driver didn't have a driver's license.

The producers dressed up OJ in gold chains and the colloquial (excuse the terminology) "wife beater" T-shirt, as if he were some sort of B-Team gangsta rapper wannabe. After being introduced to OJ, the first thing he said to me was, "Why don't you push me!" Great! I'd just met the guy who probably murdered his wife, and he wanted me to shove him.

The setup for the first supposedly "funny" prank involved singers and dancers coming in to audition for an "unnamed celebrity's" music video. What these "victims" didn't know was that the "unnamed celebrity" was actually OJ Simpson and that there was no music video.

My role, while wearing a pink belly shirt and going by the name Power, was to audition with a group of the dancers, screw things up, and then get into a big argument with OJ. So, as previously requested (and right on cue), I shoved OJ Simpson and improvised, for added effect, "Do you want a piece of me?"

I felt bad for the aspiring singers and dancers. We were wasting their time and crushing their dreams. I had expected that when OJ appeared, they would freak out and flee from the room in horror. But, as it turned out, that was not the case. The would-be performers were actually thrilled to meet OJ Simpson and hear his catchphrase: "You've been Juiced!"

Apparently, most of the duped singers and dancers thought it was great that OJ finally had the chance to show America his practical joking side. One woman, however, was not pleased with the prank and screamed, "When the ad says I'd make seven hundred fifty dollars per day, that pisses me off!" Clearly, the reward of a free *Juiced* T-shirt was not enough for her.

"Why don't you all dance around OJ," said the director to a group of excited girls. OJ attempted to be suave, adding: "This is not working out, but if you want to have dinner later, or ...?" Or what?!

Yes, OJ loved the ladies, probably a little too much. For example, while wearing a disguise and pulling a prank in a tropical-fish store, he tried his smooth tactics on a teenager by asking her, "If I were OJ, would you try to go out with me?"

The frightened girl replied, "I'm only seventeen."

OJ coyly retorted, "If you were eighteen, I'd try and go out with you!"

On the second day of production, the *Juiced* honeymoon turned rocky: there was trouble in straight-to-DVD, hidden-camera prank paradise. "OJ just doesn't give a shit," ranted the producer. "OJ shows up late. OJ doesn't want to wear wardrobe. OJ refuses to do things. What the hell is the matter with OJ?!"

As the crew, who were putting in long hours for little pay as part of OJ's big comeback attempt, impatiently waited, OJ was nowhere to be found. "It's pretty weird, you know, because of the murders," commented the sound guy, who also claimed to have sold OJ some weed. "But he is pretty funny."

Finally, a jovial OJ drove up in a golf cart. "I'm playing golf with the worst golfers," he stated to the stressed producer, who passive-aggressively pleaded with him to let the shooting begin. "I'm going to play a round of golf," OJ responded. "I need to warm up."

OJ, oblivious to the fact that roughly twenty people were waiting for him so that the filming could start, proceeded to chat away with two of his golfing buddies. After vetoing his chosen wardrobe, old-time golfing knickers (the cap was too small for his melon-sized head), things finally got rolling.

We started with a few gags—where I was supposed to once again antagonize OJ—that clearly didn't work. The humor in the gags relied heavily on OJ's less than masterful improvisational skills. For example, when I ran up to OJ, pretending to be a member of the paparazzi, he simply ignored me.

"People are always trying to catch me doing something crazy on camera," he commented to the golfers, who now wanted to pummel me silly. After quickly realizing that OJ was not blessed with the Second City art of improv, the gag ended—much to everyone's confusion—with me and the producer wrestling around on the fairway. Utilizing a phrase that never in all my life I thought possible for my brain to formulate, I informed the producer: "OJ's really not giving me much to work with!"

It was time to regroup, and OJ had a plan. He had an idea of how to really piss off his golfing buddies. After they had teed off, OJ wanted me to run onto the fairway and steal all of the golfers' balls.

"OJ! Mr. OJ! Will you sign a golf ball for me?" I yelled with flailing arms as I ran down the fairway towards the group of golfers, who emitted venomous volumes of hate through their eyes. They were pissed off to, well, OJ proportions.

One golfer, a very large and angry man, stormed directly to his golf bag and grabbed a seven iron. He cocked it back as if he were about to swing it at my head. I was depending on OJ Simpson, of all people, to protect me. In hairy situations, such as this one, he was supposed to jump in and proclaim, "You've been Juiced!" Of course, he didn't.

"PUT DOWN THE FUCKING BALL, NOW!" screamed the large and angry golfer, who was turning increasingly red as he rushed towards me with his seven iron still in hand.

"Not until OJ signs one of these golf balls," I insisted.

He demanded, again, "PUT DOWN THE FUCKING BALL, NOW!"

OJ casually commented, "That guy's crazy," acting as if he didn't know me.

Throughout the two-week production of Juiced, OJ constantly referred to me as "Crazy Boy." Seriously, how crazy does one have to be in order for OJ Simpson to refer to them as "Crazy Boy?"

The large angry man kept charging at me. So caught up in his golf game, OJ seemed to have forgotten the entire premise of the prank show. Just as the man's golf club was about to make contact with my skull, OJ nonchalantly decided to utter, before pointing to the hidden cameras, his rather important line: "You've been Juiced!" The large and angry golfer didn't give a shit.

"I DON'T CARE WHAT IT IS. YOU DON'T TOUCH PEOPLE'S BALLS!" he screamed.

Despite the prospect of a complimentary *Juiced* T-shirt, the large and angry golfer didn't calm down. "YOU JUST DON'T GO TAKING PEOPLE'S BALLS!" he continued.

After a sense of normalcy returned, OJ, while laughing, proclaimed, "I thought they were going to kick Crazy Boy's ass." Then, my eyebrow raised as OJ shared with me a self-revealing fact: "That guy was mad. He was like OJ on alcohol."

Days later, I found myself sitting with OJ in a motel room after accidentally walking in on him with his pants down. (Boxers, in case you were wondering.) As the camera crew filmed behind-the-scenes footage, another crew member applied heavy makeup to OJ's face.

"The lights are on me. I'm feeling like a star," OJ kept repeating. "I'm feeling like a star!"

For the upcoming gag, OJ was supposed to look like an old white man (with a huge head). In reality, he looked more like a severe burn victim.

Meanwhile, the television was blaring OJ's favorite channel: Court TV. OJ talked to the television as if it were a person who could hear him.

"That's such bullshit!" he kept saying to the TV.

Things turned weirdly surreal (and uncomfortable) as a Court TV reporter discussed the grizzly details of the alleged murders of Scott Peterson—that other famous guy who killed his wife. "Of course they think he's guilty," exclaimed OJ—now in complete white face—to the TV.

I prayed that the reporter wouldn't start talking about OJ. Everyone else in the room suddenly became quiet.

"How are they going to work me into this?" OJ asked the TV, with his ego seemingly in need of the added notoriety. "During my trial, my lawyers covered my ass."

The room remained quiet.

To break the tension, OJ decided to treat us with an OJ joke. "Who's the first Jewish guy to get a Heisman Trophy?" he asked. "Fred Goldman ... because he's got mine!" As everyone remained quiet (and contemplated their career choices), OJ, at the expense of the father of one of his murder victims, let out a crude laugh.

Finally, it was time to shoot the gag, which took place on bingo night at a very white Elks Club lodge. Standing under a large American flag, OJ portrayed Carl, an inept guest bingo caller with a stutter. I was on hand, dressed in a cowboy outfit, to heckle and antagonize Carl. As you can imagine, comedy mayhem ensued. OJ executed the gag with the wit and pure comedy finesse of a high school gym teacher.

While venturing back to the motel, the camera crew stopped a random guy on the street and asked if he recognized the true identity of the large-headed burn victim. When finally told it was OJ, the confused man sympathetically asked, "Is this how you have to go around now?"

Still in disguise at the end of the evening, OJ wanted to pull one more prank.

"Let's go to the bar. I want to fool my wife," he said before correcting himself. "I mean my daughter."

Always the people pleaser, OJ promised to introduce me to some key showbiz people at a production company. "You're pretty funny," he said. "You really got your stuff."

Would OJ Simpson's stamp of approval—"He comes highly recommended by OJ!"—be my fast track to the A-list? Nope. It turned out that the production company he mentioned had been out of business for over five years.

I may not have hit the big-time, but at least I was hired on for another week of *Juiced*. Now, I'm not saying that I'm that good. What I'm saying is that OJ was just that bad. In fact, a crew member shared with me his honest feelings about OJ: "It's clear that he has no talent."

For week two of *Juiced*, production moved to Las Vegas, a city of glittery facades that masks its true, vile underbelly. My goal in Vegas was to go out drinking one-on-one with OJ and see if I could get him to confess to the murders by telling him about all the murders that I had supposedly committed.

For the first "classic" prank in Vegas, OJ was to pose as a used car salesman, trying to entice unsuspecting customers to buy a white Ford Bronco that, he said ad-libbing, had "great escapability." He added, "I tried to keep mine, but unfortunately, they wouldn't let me keep it." He definitely had a sense of humor when it came to, you know, "the incident."

To make matters worse, this particular Ford Bronco, for some reason, had a large bullet hole on the side. OJ signed his name right above the hole, making the Bronco a limited edition collector's model.

"It's OJ," a man exclaimed after being pranked.

Under his breath, the man's friend laughed, "Just be glad he doesn't have a knife!"

Between pranks, while sitting in the lot manager's office, we learned more than we ever wanted to know about the famous white Bronco from the slow-speed chase.

"Ford owns Hertz. They would give me new cars each year," OJ said. "I got a Bronco and a Town Car. I gave my father-in-law the Town Car."

OJ told the producer that the police had lied about finding ten thousand dollars and had exaggerated about the amount of blood found in the Bronco. Yet, he made no mention about the disguise kit and passport the police also found.

I couldn't help feeling that OJ was only doing the straight-to-DVD production of *Juiced* strictly for the money and not for the love of hidden-camera pranks. Despite this reality, the executive producer, however, found an award-winning formula to keep OJ interested in the show. His not so brilliant idea was to keep OJ plied with alcohol. OJ took to the formula like an oversized hand to a slightly shrunken and bloody glove.

For the next gag, we set up shop in the lobby of a crappy motel off of the Vegas Strip. OJ, completely shitfaced and wearing an Elvis Presley jumpsuit, was propped up in the corner. He was supposed to play a wacky motel clerk. ("Look out! Here comes wacky motel clerk OJ. You see, it's funny because he murdered some people!") At this point, the show had devolved into the following premise: if the producers couldn't get OJ to pull the pranks, then at least they could prop up OJ somewhere near the pranks while they were being pulled.

When a hotel guest tried to check out, I was supposed to tell them their credit card had been declined, confiscate their card, and then threaten to cut it up. I know, really funny shit! Despite the enticement of a free *Juiced* T-shirt, this horrible idea resulted in people telling us to "go fuck ourselves" and storming out of the lobby. OJ, of course, failed to grasp the entire concept of the hidden-camera prank surprise.

Before I could "Juice" a couple of tourists, a drunken OJ slurred from behind his Elvis glasses, "Hey! I'm OJ!" Hey! Do you recognize me?"

The most mind-numbing part of this scenario was the fact that most tourists actually were thrilled to be in the same room as the man acquitted of double-murder. More tourists swarmed in from the Strip. Mothers and daughters requested photos.

"Oh, my God! This is the greatest thing that's ever happened to me!" screamed a kid, who high-fived his friend and then started freestyling to impress OJ. "I just rapped for OJ! That's as big as it gets!"

The final shoot of the night took place at a rented mansion

complete with topless strippers and a dancing dwarf. Things, unsurprisingly, turned sleazy: drunken OJ—wearing a pimp outfit and apparently taking a cue from the freestyling kid—started rapping. (Oh, wait, did I forget to mention that OJ recorded a rap song?)

"Yo, coach. I'm a tiger on the loose. There's no stopping the Juice," rapped OJ with the finesse of a fourth-rate Shaquille O'Neal impersonator. Some people might have seen this image as a sign of the end of the world.

Earlier in the day, while filming a prank, I spontaneously—and repeatedly—kept referring to OJ as "Danny Glover." At one point, he actually got angry: "I ALREADY TOLD YOU, I'M NOT DANNY GLOVER!" So, even before I entered into this *Entourage*-like shit show at the mansion, negative energy was already afoot. And it only got worse from there.

The guy who rented us the mansion was, on many levels, a scumbag, as were his invited buddies—large middle-aged guys with balding heads and big bellies, all of whom were slamming down copious amounts of Red Bull and vodka and getting increasingly drunk and aggressive.

How the hell do you think a night like this was going end? I knew there was going to be trouble; I just didn't know when. Do the math: OJ Simpson plus strippers plus a rented mansion plus drunken, big-bellied men. The only thing missing from this volatile mix was loaded firearms and oily rags near open flames.

When OJ's girlfriend—a heavy job title in and of itself—started flirting with me, I became nervous, especially considering the fact that OJ kept looking over at the two of us. I clearly remembered what happened to the last guy in the same situation! By no means did I want to see OJ's jealous side!

"THAT STUPID FUCKING BITCH CAN'T TALK TO ME LIKE THAT IN MY HOUSE!" interrupted an inebriated scumbag from the bathroom, where he had aggressively barged in on a stripper. Abruptly, the shoot was brought to an end, and everyone was ejected from the mansion. Of course, just when we needed him to throw down for our benefit, OJ was nowhere to be found. He had grabbed his girlfriend and snuck out.

The Vegas production came to an unexpected end as well. First thing the next morning, the producer informed me, "OJ's sick today, so we're going to pack up and go back to LA." How strange! The last time I saw OJ, he was shitfaced and pretending to be a gansta rapper.

Working on *Juiced* was like being sentenced to some sort showbiz purgatory, where everyone involved was forced to suffer the delusions of a disgraced celebrity who still craved fame but had been banished from paradise. It was a true savage journey into the heart of the American Dream, because for a brief moment, between murder charges and a lengthy prison sentence for criminal conspiracy, kidnapping, assault, robbery, and using a deadly weapon, a scandalized OJ reinvented himself as ... a zany prankster!

# THEY JUST WANNA BE LOVED

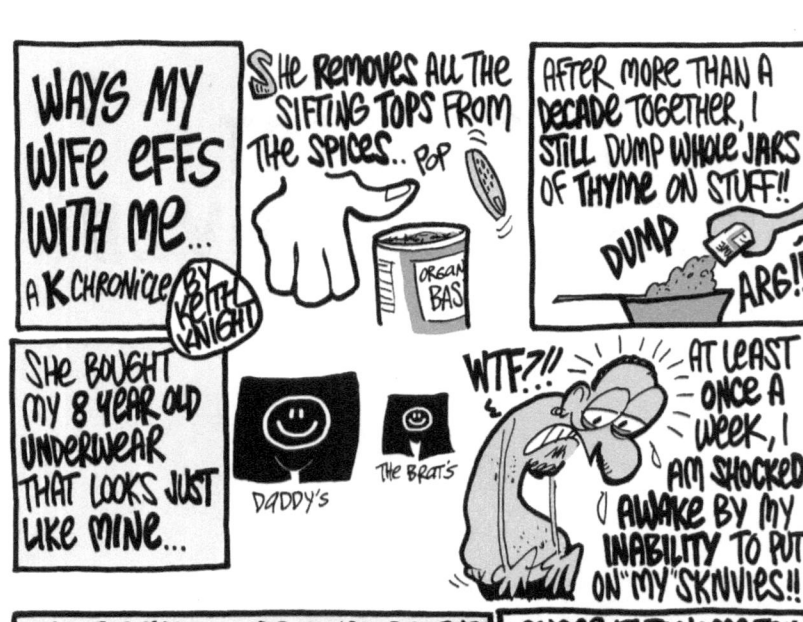

## TRIBES
Trophy Wife Hunters
Pickup Artists

## TRIBAL LEADERS
Larry Cervantes
Adam Lyons / Neil Strauss / C. Johnny Wolf / Speer

## WHERE TO SPOT TRIBE MEMBERS
AmoLatino Mail Order Bride Tour
PUA World Summit / Shopping Malls

## TRIBAL TRAITS
Men Dining and Dancing with Much Younger Women
Sarging / Uttering Provocative Pickup Lines

# TROPHY WIFE HUNTERS

A BUS FULL OF middle-aged American men—all wearing dress shirts and ironed slacks—were headed to a Latina bikini contest that was being held in a castle once owned by the textile king of Medellín, who was the first man in Colombia to be kidnapped and held for ransom. As we passed Plaza Botero, the air filled with a sense of nervousness, similar to what someone might experience if they were off to meet their future wife.

"What the fuck would I want to go to Kiev for? It's just a nuclear plant right next to Chernobyl," exclaimed Earl from Oregon in a rant about international dating tours, where American men were sometimes inclined to propose marriage to foreign women that they had met just earlier in the day. "Russia is run by the Mafia. You're not always chatting with the girl in the profile."

Earl looked like a guy who had done some hard living. In fact, he boasted about being a former heroin addict and a stockbroker, claiming that he once lost a million dollars in a single day. A silent Colombian woman sat next to Earl. A few days later, she would be his wife, even though neither of them spoke the other's language.

For many years, Medellín, Colombia was considered one of the ten most dangerous tourist destinations in the world. But despite the possible peril, these men had paid almost sixteen hundred dollars (plus airfare) to fly to the City of Eternal Spring for the AmoLatino mail order bride tour. The company's literature trumpeted the six-day romance excursion as "the ultimate guys' holiday," where "very beautiful women who are intrigued by you" are "a bonus."

According to Larry Cervantes, who organized the mail order bride tour from an office in Moscow, the men had signed-up for a variety of reasons, ranging from marriage to carnal lust. "Everyone has something they're after, and we understand that," he said. And Larry should know. Similar to the head of the Hair Club for Men, not only was Larry the tour organizer, he was also a former client.

To kick things off, twenty-four American men gathered in a conference room on the second floor of the Hotel Dann Carlton for the morning briefing.

"You gentlemen are about to join a select group of guys who have already experienced what you are about to experience," Larry said to the anxious group. The brood of trophy bride seekers ran life's gauntlet: middle-aged men who were divorced (sometimes two or three times), widowed, or never married. Some of these wealthy men—finance guys, real estate agents, oil industry engineers, ex-military—even had grown children, from whom they wanted to keep this romance adventure secret.

"You won't find the numbers you will when you come back to the U.S. Colombia is a place with an enormous amount of beautiful women. We tapped into it," said Larry, before mentioning that there must be something in the Columbian water. His attempt at humor received big laughs from the eager men.

Conversely, Larry warned: "This isn't a tourist town. Be aware of your surroundings. This city has a history for a reason!"

As I opened my AmoLatino orientation book and noticed important Spanish phrases to memorize—"I love you and only you" (*Te quiero a ti y solamente a ti*) and "You drive me crazy" (*Me vuelves loco*)—I wondered if finding a mail order bride might cost someone his life!

Like the General Patton of romance tours, Larry continued his diatribe while the men diligently took notes. "Dress as best as you can. This is a big deal for a lot of the ladies. You represent their possible future mate," he instructed. "Be the man and take control of the situation."

In past tours, when the man didn't take control, problems arose. For example, if the woman was allowed to choose the restaurant, then the man often found her entourage suddenly growing to include her neighbors, relatives, and extended family. Or if the man momentarily stepped away from the table, he might return only to discover that a bottle of Dom Pérignon had magically appeared.

"When you're out, it's all on your dime," Larry stressed. "Once again, be in control! The lady doesn't get the choice!"

In my notebook, I scrawled: "Take control of situation."

Before the American troops were cut loose on foreign soil, Larry had some final words. "My team is here to help you set up individual dates, meet girls," he said while gesturing to the two lovely, young Russian women by his side, "and have a good experience."

As the men stood up, ready to start their quests, Larry added, "This is a grand Shangri-La of women. Happy hunting! Find your princess!"

In my notebook, I scrawled: "Find your princess!"

Barry, an oil company engineer, looked around the room at the surreal sight. "I've been chatting to a couple of girls online. They both showed up," he said with childlike excitement. Although he had not yet met either of the women in person, the fact that he had trekked from Virginia to Medellín weighed in his corner: "It indicates that I'm serious."

A large queue of *muchachas*—mostly in their late teens and early twenties—checked in at the registration desk. Dressed in their nightclub best, these four hundred eighty women had registered for the night's social at Mangos, a Wild West themed nightclub in the heart of Medellín. At the club, which felt like a fantasy baseball camp for middle-aged gents, table after table was filled with beautiful Colombian women. It was as if this reality, where young Latino maidens pursued the loins of older men from faraway lands, existed in a parallel universe.

"You think it would be competitive, but there's so many women here," Barry said with a smile.

As the energy of the frenzied club swelled, paunchy American men—fueled by Club Colombia beer and free tequila shots—attempted to do the booty dance.

"Don't lock in too early. The lady will try and occupy your time," said Larry, trying to provide some last minute advice to a pack of guys. "You want to move around the room. Don't spend too much time at one table."

On the prowl for their Colombian trophy wives, the sharks circled the cage as an estrogen-charged fervor—normally reserved for Chippendales dancers—was directed towards the twenty-four men on the AmoLatino tour. Bart—a gray-haired, retired high school principal—took his place at a table with four women, holding court as if he were royalty … or MC Hammer.

The insane ratio of women to men (twenty-to-one) had left the majority of women unattended. As the courting ritual between the older American men with money and the fertile, young Latinas continued, the room ran the course of life's emotions: expectations, optimism, boredom, and doubt.

Then, it got real: two hunky shirtless guys covered in oil suddenly appeared on top of the bar, gyrating to the club music and working up the ladies to screams of delight. Next, out came the booty dance and a dancing dwarf, who, for some odd reason, was still considered funny by Colombian culture.

Larry advised that if you saw a girl with whom you wanted to connect, ask one of the translators, a group of lovely Medellín college girls, to make an introduction since the girl might not speak English. Not to overshadow someone's potential future wife, the translators were instructed not to wear anything provocative. "A good translator does a great job at playing wingman," Barry said. "They kind of break the ice and talk you up—that sort of thing."

Typical phrases that needed translation included: "do you have children?" "are you married?" and "you have lovely teeth."

Some translators changed the meaning of the men's words. For example, one of the guys wanted to ask a woman to stand up and do the booty dance. "I just didn't think it was appropriate," explained our table's translator.

"Why do you think a lot of the women are here?" I asked her.

"In Colombia, everyone from outside is seen as better," she said, attempting to explain her country's prevalent low self-esteem. "Better jobs. Better money. Better life. It's an opportunity to move to America."

While a few guys lingered around the room like high school social studies teachers at prom, the oily muscular duo continued to gyrate. Was this pair of dancers the physical ideal for the majority of women here? Had social-economic circumstances forced them to settle for less attractive options? For the young Colombian women, the older men represented security. And for the men, the women embodied the prospect of not dying alone. Everyone had their needs.

I stood at the bar with Adrian, who ditched his life as a British diplomat to run the local AmoLatino office. On stage, a line of women took turns doing an overly sexualized dance that involved squatting near a phallic-shaped, upright beer bottle. Was one of them the future Mrs. Leon? "We're selling happiness," Adrian said as an older woman's gyrating squat thrusts put her younger competition to shame. "I can't think of anything more satisfying."

As the social winded down, the young, fertile women had worn out these guys, including the dancing dwarf, who lingered alone in the corner. The men left in the same manner they had arrived: in packs. Like war victims in the aftermath of a bomb explosion, the few remaining men staggered around the room (dazed, disorientated, and confused), trying to make last minute connections with women. But they were contorted with drunkenness and moved around the club as if they were suffering from amorous, post-traumatic stress disorder.

The next day, the scene at the castle, an ornate villa nestled on the side of a hill, was breathtaking. The James Bond fantasy for the men continued with a female-heavy social inside a room with white couches. Hors d'oeuvres were served and punch flowed. Droves of women walked past a fountain filled with red rose pedals. Below, Medellín's outstretching valley sparkled like a rare fruit.

Surrounded by cameras, Earl, the former stockbroker who lost one million dollars in a single day, was playing media darling. Television giants Telemundo and Univision were on hand to cover the night's festivities, and Earl's upcoming marriage had made him a tour success story.

"I like the most in a woman to reflect me—like a mirror," Earl said with raspy voice as he placed his hand in front of his face, miming a mirror. "I believe everyone reflects everyone else in life."

While that sentiment may have been true, his future wife stood by his side, not understanding a single damn word he said.

The evening's social was combined with a beauty pageant that featured women who had signed-up on the AmoLatino dating website. Its purpose: to prove that these beautiful women were real by having them put on their smallest bikinis and parade around in front of their future potential husbands to prove it.

Hundreds of attendees filtered into the main room for the commencement of the big event.

From the stage, Larry proclaimed, "This is AmoLatino's inaugural Miss Colombia beauty pageant." His words were translated into Spanish for the audience.

The beauty contest was judged by an astute panel of experts: three guys from the mail order bride tour and an eye-candy-tastic Colombian TV celebrity.

I snuck backstage, where it was a hustle and bustle of costume changes and shouts of "*muchachas!*" Large men in nice suits helped the beauty contestants—fierce contenders with husbands in their eyes—on stage. There was Christina (the bad girl in red), Rosalita (with fire in her eyes), and Scarlet (oh, sweet Scarlet). Men with sweaty brows looked on as the women were presented wearing different clothes.

"*Plastico,*" exclaimed Telemundo reporter Isabel Ramirez

when the contestants reemerged wearing tiny bikinis. Since many consider Colombia the plastic surgery capital of the world, fake boobs abounded and uplifted booties defied the laws of physics.

"Colombian women are very natural, beautiful women. But here, you look, big bumps," she said to me, referring to the sea of artificial implants.

Perhaps Isabel was failing to see the larger picture: the necessity of wife-seeking men to see their potential bride first in a bikini and high heels before being judged by a panel of strangers.

"These aren't women; they're girls ... babies ... eighteen years old," Isabel said, referring to the pageant contestants. "You can see sadness in their eyes."

I asked if the sadness stemmed from the fact that many of the women came from the poor sections of Medellín, such as the slums of Santo Domingo.

"I don't think these women are poor. These are women who want it easy," she theorized. "I spoke with some of the ladies. They don't want a husband. They don't want babies. These girls want money and luxury and travel. Not love.

"In Colombia, we have a big problem with narcotraffic. The narcotraffic changed the dreams of Colombian women."

Isabel explained that narcotrafficking had created a superficial mentality amongst a certain type of women in local society. "They want to get money for big bumps!" she exclaimed. "If you want a good wife, you don't put her in a little dress. You don't find her at a beauty pageant—not your wife, not the mother of your babies."

The pageant was narrowed down to the five finalists. Through a translator, the contestants were asked to describe their perfect man. A woman responded, via translation, "I want a man who will make me feel like a princess."

The next question: "Where will you be in five years?"

Translated answer: "I want to change the world ... or be a publicist."

To crying and a sea of confetti, the winner of the mail order bride beauty pageant was announced. The brown-haired beauty was awarded a brand new motorbike. Personally, I was disappointed that Ed McMahon did not come back from the dead to hand out one of those really large checks.

I half-expected the winner to be married right on stage while strains of "The Star-Spangled Banner" rang throughout the room and American dollar bills rained from the ceiling. Instead, the translator interpreted her words: "She is happy and surprised."

The next morning, Earl looked bleary-eyed and wrecked, as if he had spent a week in the jungle snorting bumps of coke off a Bowie knife. "I did eight shots of vodka last night," he declared. "And they were double shots."

We walked down the hallway towards the lobby, and I asked him, "Did you have fun being interviewed on Colombian TV?"

Flashing paranoia, Earl replied, "I don't know how cool that was."

I asked, "Why?"

He seemed worried: "Because I'm an American saying I'm marrying a Colombian woman on TV."

I questioned him, "What's the worst case scenario?"

He immediately answered, "I'd get killed or kidnapped."

After a moment's pause, I replied, "Let's hope that doesn't happen."

In the lobby, a theater of the uncomfortable was being acted out as a dozen men waited for their dates—most of whom they had never met—to show up. Some of the women were flying in from other cities. When they finally arrived, awkward body language and forced interactions ensued. A sad play—followed by uncomfortable silences—unfolded as guys attempted to hold women's hands. Everyone's backstory was written clearly on their faces.

But luck was better for gray-haired Bart. Over the course of the tour, he had been on twenty dates. In fact, a forty-year-old woman with whom he had a tryst wanted to set him up with her twenty-year-old daughter.

The brain center of international dating was situated in a hospitality suite on the hotel's fifth floor. If a man on the tour wanted a date, he simply asked the fifth floor Russian women (just like the village matchmakers in *Fiddler on the Roof*), and it was arranged.

"A bunch of the guys are meeting for drinks at Hooters," said Barry, asking me if I'd like to join the group. I told him I couldn't because I had a date.

Before arriving at the brain center for further instructions, I visited the AmoLatino website and searched the words "artist," "journalist," and "bikini model." The result: about a dozen stunning woman—all of whom looked as if their photos were taken at the same glamour studio—popped up on the page. Just like ordering used car parts off of eBay, I simply selected and made a list of the five women I wanted to date, and it was automatically set up.

"Barry is going home tomorrow," the Russian matchmaker said over the phone to a representative at the local agency. "He wants to send chocolates for Lady Diana. Can he send it to your office?"

Bart, who sat on the couch, was being briefed about his dates. "The lady who is coming tonight has two kids," he was told. "And the eighteen-year-old, she has accepted your date as well."

He provided me with more details: "She's eighteen years old, so her mom is coming with because she's still a virgin. The other one has kids, so I'm not really interested because I can get that back home."

While looking at my list of potential wives, my Russian matchmaker said, "Tonight, you have a date at eight."

I didn't know what to expect. All I knew was that I was the man and needed to take charge! The previous night, Brady didn't take charge. At a restaurant of her choosing, he met the teenaged girl with whom he had been corresponding via email. She brought along her mom, sister, nephew, and a neighbor: "The gringo is in town. Everyone, let's eat!" Brady had to flip the bill for the entire party, including a translator: the teenager, of course, couldn't speak English.

Outside the local dating agency office, which was near Parque San Antonio, I waited for my date, Christina, with my trusty translator by my side. My date was thirty minutes late, and I had butterflies in my stomach. Why was I nervous? It was a strange sensation that

I had never experienced. What if someone whom I had never met rejected me?

Finally, a cab pulled up. My potential future wife was inside. Christina, a very attractive blonde, was wearing a low cut dress. Was she the one? How many international weddings had been instigated with those exact feelings?

"Let's go for drinks!" I suggested with a smile.

After a few minutes of conferring with my translator, it was determined that she wanted dinner.

Okay. If that was the case, then I needed to be the man and take charge by choosing the restaurant.

"She wants to go for Italian food," my translator relayed.

Sure, she could choose the restaurant, but I was the man who was taking charge. Christina ordered a full meal; I ordered soup. Fifteen minutes into the date, her cell phone rang. She stayed on the phone for the next ten minutes, talking rapidly in Spanish and leaving me to swirl my spoon in my soup.

What followed was the awkwardness of a blind date mixed with the fact that we were unable to communicate directly—all small talk was filtered through a third-party translator with a several minute lag between responses. It was agreed that we both liked music. There were big laughs. A momentary connection was made over both of us having seen the same movie. I could only imagine the small talk Brady must have made when he took an entire family out on a blind date. Was this how most good marriages started?

Christina was very pleasant and attractive, but we literally couldn't communicate, and the punchlines to all my jokes were lost in translation. For the majority of the long two-hour date, I ended up talking to my translator. And even if Christina and I had hit it off, I was returning to America the next day. Unfortunately, that pretty much left just that night for getting married. I wondered what married life back in the United States would be like without a translator tagging along. Once the bill was paid, Christina abruptly wanted to go home. Wedding bells had to wait.

"You need to give her sixty thousand pesos for her cab ride

home," stated my translator.

I felt strange about handing over handfuls of money to my date. If somehow sex had been involved, then these rules of attraction would have made more sense. Instead, it was just an evening spent between two people who couldn't speak the same language and who strained to carry on a conversation through a third party translator.

"She liked you. I could tell," said my translator as her cab pulled away.

That was nice to hear. But why did I feel slightly creepy, a little bit sad, and all alone? When it came to the rules of attraction conspiring with an American globalization twist, was it really love? Or was it just a free ticket to the land of Coca Cola and Donald Trump? I honestly didn't know as I glanced at a table of stunning women who were dining at an outdoor restaurant—and laughing to the beat of life—in this truly heartbreaking and beautiful world.

# PICKUP ARTISTS

Level 3 Nightclub in Hollywood was filled with some of the world's top pickup artists: Hypnotica, Bad Boy, Hydro, and Adoni. Apparently, these amour gurus went by ridiculous monikers in order to sound more intriguing when "sarging," the process of trying to secure strange women's phone numbers for the purpose of convincing the women to have sex with them. At the fourth annual PUA (Pickup Artist) World Summit, approximately three hundred eager alpha males—from playas to normal accountant-looking types—had assembled to usher in a new era of mastery in the art of picking up women.

"That dick isn't going to suck itself!" exclaimed a PUA instructor to the large gathering of men. In turn, the PUA Summit participants sprung to their feet and in unison chanted: "IT'S GOING TO GET BETTER! IT'S GOING TO GET BETTER!"

Welcome to the cult of the pickup artist, a pickle party of playa mastery that had attracted men from the far reaches of the world, including Croatia, Germany, Australia, and China. These eager men had all paid hundreds of dollars to learn advanced techniques from the professionals of the "seduction community" in order to gain confidence and transform from sexless nobodies into masters of attraction.

During the summit, the laws of pickup artist mastery were to be broken down into a clear, calculated science that PUAs could apply to real life. In this new era of pickup artistry, progressive PUAs had deserted the Mystery Method—which was outline in the 2005 Neil Strauss book *The Game: Penetrating the Secret Society of Pickup Artists*—and no longer employed a set of props and magic tricks while "peacocking" in large, funny hats. These raconteurs of seduction secured women's phone numbers by creating an opening in the immediate moment, escalating the situation, and then closing the deal, because as their Sensei just mentioned, "That dick isn't going to suck itself!"

Much like the haggard salesmen in *Glengarry Glen Ross*, PUAs instructed their pupils to practice the ABCs (Always Be Closing.) "You are selling people; you are selling yourself," explained Adam Lyons, considered to be one of the best PAUs in the world. A member of the London Seduction Society, Lyons, at the peak of his career, claimed to have been accompanied to clubs by twenty or thirty good looking women.

According to Lyons, men, when "sarging," should never go more than ten seconds without "opening a set" with a woman. He advised PAUs to step up "like real men" and make the commitment.

"Make yourself become a better person," suggested Lyons. "You got to have a good product so a woman will give you five minutes of their time. Being afraid of rejection only creates anxiety and blue balls."

Lyons suggested that instead of memorizing a bunch of pickup lines, guys must forget about appearing needy or desperate and work on developing confidence and positive character traits in order to become the men that women desire. According to Lyons, simple things, such as asking directions, making an interesting observation, or paying a compliment worked best.

"Once the opener goes well, isolate and escalate!" Lyons told the crowd. He suggested following up with a transition line: "Where are you from? You are so friendly."

Sure, it would have been easy to write off most of these guys, with their preprogrammed and rehearsed lines, as nothing but sleazy, trained predators—if it weren't for the fact that some were just ordinary, shy guys trying to muster the courage to ask women on dates.

For example, Neil Strauss, author of *The Game*, grew up as a scrawny kid who was bullied by his classmates. At age fifteen, he already was certain that he would live his entire life without ever having sex. In high school, Strauss and a group of his similarly misfit friends called themselves the "V Club"—because all of them were virgins.

Things changed for Strauss—and the rest of the PUA world—in 2000 with the online publication of the *How to Lay Girls Guide*. Inspired, he signed up for a workshop with Erik von Markovik, more popularly known by his stage name, Mystery, who hosted a short-lived VH1 reality show (aptly titled *The Pickup Artist*) and authored the book *The Mystery Method: How to Get Beautiful Women Into Bed*. Mystery then befriended Strauss and made him his wingman.

Reinvented with the alter-ego "Style," Strauss, with Mystery and a group of other pickup artists, moved in the Project Hollywood house, a mansion where they worked on mastering pickup techniques. While they became masters at acquiring women's phone numbers, none, however, were able to attract a girlfriend. Overcoming this problem is where the PUA Summit aims to provide guidance: what to do once a man has a woman's phone number.

So, in addition to utilizing the ABCs, instructors at the summit also advised PUAs to engage in the ABTs (Always Be Touching), which should raise an eye in the current #MeToo movement that has brought down many serial sexual harassers. But this didn't seem to serve as a deterrent to the pickup artists, who were mentored to establish touching with the woman early in "the set."

While conversing with women, PUAs were told to instigate light touches and squeezes and subsequently escalate the situation if the women seemed responsive. Hugging and palm reading, the PUAs were told, served as other good ways to test the physical contact waters. Apparently, it didn't matter that going from absolutely no physical contact to suddenly touching women might come across as creepy, not to mention borderline illegal.

In fact, Always Be Touching didn't work out so well for Julien Blanc, an American pickup artist who was banned from entering the UK, where he planned to hold a PUA boot camp. YouTube clips showed Blanc shoving women's faces into his crotch and inappropriately kissing an unsuspecting Japanese checkout clerk. Another video showed Blanc, at one of his seduction boot camps, sharing an anecdote on Japanese women: "If you're a white male, you can do what you want. I'm just romping through the streets, just grabbing girls' heads, just like, head, pfft, on the dick."

After more than one hundred fifty thousand people signed a petition accusing Blanc of promoting sexual assault at his seduction seminars, authorities denied his visa application.

It makes one wonder why the current U.S. President, who was captured on tape bragging about how he likes to grab women by the pussy, was not also banned from entering the UK.

Billed as the senior instructor for the ABCs of Attraction, the questionably named C. Johnny Wolf, founder of the California Lair of Pickup Artists, philosophized on his simple secret with the ladies: "All you got to do is be happy. If you're happy with your life, it will come naturally."

To illustrate this happiness and thus inspire the PUAs, a video was shown that included footage of Wolf swimming with sharks, venturing into a cave that was infested with flying bats, and knocking out an opponent while Thai boxing.

"It's time to liberate yourself from all the bullshit and walk towards your passion and what you want in life," Wolf said to the crowd in a call for action. "When you see a girl at a club, don't hesitate. Start walking towards your goal. If you don't know the exact opening line to say, you'll figure it out in the moment."

Following his diatribe, more Alpha male testosterone-fueled chanting filled the room as the PUAs in unison were coerced to chant: "IF I DO SOMETHING, I'LL FIGURE IT OUT! IF I DO

SOMETHING, I'LL FIGURE IT OUT!"

When the chanting died down, Wolf added: "Five to ten years from now, I want to see a wedding invitation from all of you guys." At least he wanted his pupils to be married and not part of the sex offender registry.

As the afternoon dragged on, the attendees were presented with more socially archaic ideas from Michael Hurst, author of *Become That Guy: Become Irresistibly Attractive*, who let the crowd in on a bit of "insider" information: "Know that women want sex!" He said that operating under this premise while using his direct approach has helped him bed both party girls and virgins—and even led to him receiving a hummer in an airplane bathroom.

Vince Kelvin, PUA Summit co-founder and author of *Same Night Sex*, who claimed to have slept with no fewer than twenty-seven porn stars, offered more of the same bad advice. "Look, the Kool-Aid man doesn't just come to your door and whisper, 'Kool Aid.' No," he said. "The Kool-Aid man breaks right through the goddamn wall."

According to Kelvin's theory, sexual talk entices women to start thinking about bumping uglies. "Present sex to women as superior behavior," he advocated.

Clad in bracelets and necklaces and sporting a business card that was printed on a condom wrapper, Kelvin suggested that it was necessary to rebrand slutty women as sexually liberated and powerful women by using aggressive words as part of provocative sentences: "What's the most interesting place you have had sex?" or "Let's go! I'm a guy, and I want to fuck you."

If only it were that simple! In reality, if a man uttered those lines to a complete stranger, the result would be a drink thrown in their eyes.

With the summit complete, it was time to observe PUA techniques in the real world. I joined Miami PUA Speer at a shopping mall on Hollywood Boulevard for his mini boot camp.

His pupil, a twenty-two-year-old named Caesar, looked petrified. "There's a two-set," Speer said to Caesar while pointing out a pair of women who were dining at a table. "Remember, it's sitting and asking all in one motion."

As an opener, Speer, who had devised a patented way (the "Speer Method") to approach women, instructed Caesar to bait one of the women with an opinion so that she would invest in the conversation. A hesitant (and nervous) Caesar finally jumped into action. As coached, he sat down at the table with relaxed body posture—a position of power—and engaged one of the women in conversation. Soon, the woman was smiling.

"She's turned in. That's an indicator of interest," Speer pointed out to me. "At this time, he should get the number."

Success!

Caesar returned to Speer all smiles. "She gave me her number," he proclaimed. "She's from South Africa and wanted to find stuff to do."

Speer had some feedback for young Caesar. "Next time, be sure to interact with her friend," he advised. "Don't ask a lot of questions. No one likes to be interviewed. Show them you have a personality and can lead a conversation."

It was time for a more challenging phase two: pick up a woman while she was walking. "Do you know how to do moving sets?" Speer asked his protégé.

Caesar anxiously nodded his head. The key, according to the Speer Method, was for Caesar to position himself directly in front of his target and then turn around. "Have a picture on your cell phone, walk in front of the girl, turn, and say, 'I was at this club, and my phone dropped. Has that happened to you?'" instructed Speer.

"I'll open those two," said Caesar as he bolted past a pair of blonds before turning around in front of them. It didn't work; they kept walking.

"They were cool, but I couldn't get them to stop," said Caesar, feeling dejected.

"Just keep tossing it out until they hook," advised Speer. "Keep moving. Then, go direct!"

Caesar gave it another shot; he succeeded by persuading a

brunette woman to stop. Now confident, he opted to pull a classic PUA maneuver: cutting out of the conversation and then, moments later, turning back to the woman.

"He just did a *Columbo*, announced Speer, who was beaming with pride. "It's taking yourself out of the set and then turning back."

Caesar was also happy with his success: "Every day, I go to the park and try to get numbers."

Speer used to do the same, only at a mall, which was where he achieved one of the true goals of the professional pickup artist: acquiring a steady girlfriend. "A relationship is the longest set you are going to have for life," he admitted. "You always got to keep things new and exciting."

Maybe in five to ten years, Speer would make C. Johnny Wolf proud with a wedding invitation. After all, no one wants to die alone—or at least not without a pocket full of phone numbers.

# THEIR TRIBES ARE CULTS

## TRIBES
The Raëlians
Staring Cult

## TRIBAL LEADERS
Raël the Race Car Driver
John de Ruiter

## WHERE TO SPOT TRIBE MEMBERS
Space Welcome Embassy / Bowling Alleys
The Oasis Center / International Seminars

## TRIBAL TRAITS
Watching for Extraterrestrials / Wearing Infinity Symbols
Staring at a Silent Man / Engaging in Misattribution

# THE RAËLIANS

THE SIGN CAUGHT MY eye … or maybe it was the sexy French woman who boasted ample cleavage. I'm not really sure. "All life on earth, including human beings, was originally created scientifically in laboratories by the Elohim, an advanced people from space!" said the woman in an attempt to lure me to the Raëlian booth.

And it worked. "Tell me more!" I replied, still wondering to myself why I had chosen to infiltrate a new age convention in San Francisco called "A Gathering of Light."

"The only person the Elohim communicate with is Raël," she explained, with sincere conviction, in her enticing French accent.

While taking my eyes off of the French woman for a moment and glancing down at Raëlian table, I noticed several copies of their book, *Message from Extraterrestrials*. On the back cover of the book was a photo of Raël, an older French man sporting a ponytail. I noted that before becoming the head of his eponymous cult, Raël was race car driver! I would have bet good money that I was talking to Raël's woman.

"Didn't Raël use to be a race car driver?" I inquired, trying to get on her good side.

"Aah, do you know Raël?" she excitedly asked before explaining the Raëlian religion's mission: building a twenty million dollar space embassy to entice the return of the aliens. It was just like *Field of Dreams* ("If you build it, they will come."), except this was a twenty million dollar space embassy and not a baseball diamond in the middle of an Iowa cornfield.

"An embassy?!" I repeated.

She then showed me an artist's rendition of the embassy, which looked like an elongated and futuristic white igloo.

"Yes, that's a nice space embassy," I confirmed.

There was nothing wrong with Raël's dream. Hell, if I were a rich race car driver, I, too, might start my own religious sect and name it ... after myself! And the Harmonian religion, of course, would recruit sexy French female followers. "Rock on Raël," I thought.

I'm not sure if it was the magnetism of Raël's author photo on the back of the book (or the shapely buttocks of the French woman working the Raëlian booth), but soon I had booked a plane ticket to Montreal, the home of the headquarters of the Raëlian religion.

I always have been distrustful of religions. For the most part, they are nothing but cults designed to manipulate their followers. But perhaps a religion with a science fiction theme and a race car driver-prophet was more up my alley.

Through the Raëlian website (ww.rael.org), I located their headquarters and planned to attend one of their weekly organizational meeting. Yes, I was prepared to sit in a large room filled with other Raëlian recruits and learn about the mysteries of a sci-fi religion. My expectations were at a level where I anticipated the insanity itself would be enough to make Scientology, a cult created by a science fiction writer, seem Amish in comparison.

Since *ET* is my favorite sci-fi movie, I selected the appropriate undercover pseudonym of Elliot Spielberg, which I thought would help me get into character. As Elliot, I dressed up like a seventh grade science teacher, complete in white short-sleeve shirt and clip-on tie. But for my cover to work, I needed a backstory: Elliot hailed from Moosejaw, Canada, where, as a child, he had an alien encounter during a family barbecue. Finally, I was ready to meet the Raëlians.

Their headquarters was located off of St. Laurent on the second floor of a warehouse that also housed a discount futon outlet. Someone in Montreal told me that this was the place where the Raëlians held wild sex parties filled with beautiful French women. Though I didn't believe that humans were created in a laboratory by space aliens, I did appreciate the possibility of having unattached sex with French hotties. A little paranoid about the Raëlian encounter, I was sure to let others know where I was going to be in case I didn't return within a reasonable time frame.

After a few knocks, a door—with a picture of a large alien head—invitingly swung open. The turnout for the 7:30 p.m. weekly meeting was less stellar than I expected. Inside the large warehouse-like room, which was scattered with paintings of aliens in various states of alien-ness, two sad-looking men sat on couches. They seemed surprised at the emergence of another attendee.

"I'm here for the Raëlian meeting," I stated, wondering where in the hell the hot French women were.

One of the men, who sported a Michael Bolton haircut and wore a vest with no shirt underneath, signaled for me to sit down next to him. Instead, I made my way for the couch farthest from him. For some strange reason, I had the uneasy feeling that he might try to touch me in an inappropriate alien way. As a result, I held tightly onto my Dr. Pepper can in case I needed it as a makeshift weapon.

The other man bore a striking resemblance to an elf and/or space alien. He remained silent while staring straight ahead.

Then, the strong and glassy eye contact began.

"Did you come all the way to Montreal to meet with the Raëlians?" asked the Michael Bolton doppelgänger in a thick French accent.

I turned the tables on him. "Yes! Growing up, I've had many encounters with UFOs. The last was at a family barbecue. I thought this might be the place for me," I informed. "Plus, I'm really into race car driving." I concluded by spewing out all the Raëlian trivia I learned on their website.

"This is not a group for spotting UFOs," retorted Michael Bolton before explaining that the Raëlian organization has over five thousand members in Montreal.

Both he and the elf wore around their necks a symbol that resembled the Star of David but contained outer space stuff in the middle.

"It's the 'Symbol of Infinity,'" explained Bolton. Apparently, the insignia once had a swastika in the middle, but for some odd reason, the majority of people didn't respond favorably to it. So, it was removed.

As the elf continued to stare straight ahead, a large screen, situated between two "artistic" banners of women showing their backsides, began to project a video: *The True Face of God*. With special effects obviously created by an Amiga video toaster from the late 1980s, the movie attempted to show us what the "true face of God" might look like (if God had appeared in an old *Dr. Who* episode).

Next in the video, the author of the book *Fingerprints of the Gods* lectured us about the word "Elohim," claiming that it was misinterpreted as "God" in the Bible. What a craaaaazy oversight. Good thing the man in the video looked like a scientist. Otherwise, he would have had no credibility. His presentation continued with many vague references to space aliens located within the Holy Scriptures.

"All history books would have to be changed," the scientist explained, letting us in on why the media conceals the fact that we evolved from a master race of aliens.

Then, there was a reenactment with an actor portraying a young Raël during his first encounter with a UFO.

"In 1975, Raël was taken back to the Elohim planet," informed Michael Bolton while attempting to invade my personal space.

"Wow, how long did it take to do that?" I asked.

"Two and a half hours!" he exclaimed.

"That's amazing!" I said. "When aliens took me back to their home planet, it took over three days."

Michael Bolton seemed unimpressed. So was the elf, who still stared straight ahead.

"When will the Space Welcome Embassy be built?" I asked.

"2035!" proclaimed Bolton with certainty.

"Why not sooner?" I asked, rather puzzled.

"We could build it sooner, but by 2035, technology will be advanced enough that humans will be able to understand it," rationalized Bolton.

So, in essence, Michael Bolton was saying that if they built the Space Welcome Embassy now, the human race would be unable to comprehend it. Or, perhaps, a better theory might be that if the Elohim DIDN'T return after the Raëlians spent twenty million dollars building a Space Welcome Embassy, then Raël would be left with extraterrestrial egg on his face.

My paranoia increased when two more Raëlians peered out from behind a partially cracked door. Were my many years of kickboxing training about to be necessary to defend myself? Fortunately, they disappeared behind the door. The elf stared ahead, and Michael Bolton kept shifting on the couch while looking at me.

"In all religions, there's one prophet who returns to earth. We believe it is Raël," said Bolton.

"So what you're saying is that all of the prophets of each religion have been mistaken for the Elohim?" I asked.

"YES!" he replied.

"And the reason Raël was visited by a UFO is because he is a prophet?" I inquired.

"YES!!" said Bolton.

It was time, once again, to turn the tables. I puffed out my chest and insinuated that I, too, might be a prophet, possibly even their new Messiah! I proclaimed, "Maybe the reason why I had an encounter with a UFO is that, perhaps, they came special to see me!"

Michael Bolton looked aghast. Even the elf glanced over at me.

"NO! Raël is the only prophet on Earth. Raël is the last prophet!" exclaimed Bolton.

"You never know," I said, giving my best I-might-be-your-new-

Messiah smile.

On that note, Michael Bolton quickly wrapped up things but not before inviting me to their weekly Raëlian gathering. That's right, Raëlian bowling night.

"You'll have fun," he stated. "We're a little crazy!"

That was the understatement of the millennium.

"How will I be able to find you?" I asked.

In unison, both he and the elf held up their Symbols of Infinity.

"Just look for this!" Bolton instructed.

Oh yeah, of course.

I was excited about the prospect of bowling with Raëlians. So, that night I was off to a place in Montreal called Jillian's, which turned out to be the coolest bowling alley I had ever seen. At the end of each lane, large video screens played music videos as bowlers threw multi-colored balls under florescent lights. The French-Canadians knew how to make even bowling seem chic!

However, none of the groups of happy bowlers appeared to be wearing the Symbol of Infinity.

"Raëlians?!" I yelled, attempting to get the attention of anyone willing to usher me into a little game of ten-pin.

After gathering some courage, I approached a woman who was about to roll a ball.

"Excuse me, but are you a Raëlian?" I asked.

She looked at me as if I had just pooped my pants and was asking for a hug. I took that as a "no."

So, I decided to phone home—to the Raëlians that is—and reached a recorded message: "You have reached the Raëlian religion. Stay on the line. Someone will answer to you."

Moments later, a French woman, who spoke broken English, answered. I told her that Michael Bolton and the elf invited me to Raëlian bowling night at Jillian's but that I did not see anyone with the Symbol of Infinity. She assured me that the Raëlians were there and told me to call back in ten minutes. I thought I heard giggling in the background. Ten minutes later, I called back, but no one answered the phone.

Apparently, I had been stood up by the Raëlians ... at a bowling alley! Not a lonelier feeling in the universe existed. At the very least they could have cloned some members and sent their asses down here in bowling shoes?!

Then it hit me: the Raëlians were having a big sex orgy back at the headquarters, and I was sent bowling. It seemed as if the Raëlians had two doors for new members—one for those who got to participate in sex orgies and the other for those who were sent bowling. I guess I did not make the cut!

I wondered if Jesus or Buddha would have deserted one of their potential disciples and left them alone at a bowling alley, crushed, with pins still in formation and rented shoes on their feet.

I looked toward the heavens—onto the next solar system—and spat!

There was NO cloned God!

# STARING CULT

JOHN DE RUITER (OR simply "John" to his followers) sat in a large armchair on an elevated stage in front of a packed auditorium. Every person in the entire room was focused on him and the intense gaze emanating from his steely blue eyes. Mammoth video screens on both sides of the stage projected an extreme close-up of John's handsome face, which looked like that of a top-tier Porsche salesman. For the next hour, we silently stared at John as if he were the L. Ron Hubbard of staring.

His followers, who number in the thousands, consider John the "living embodiment of truth." During his three-hour staring sessions, or "meetings" as they are called, John's devotees have claimed that they can see an aura around him. Some followers believe that John can look straight into a person's soul.

Before he founded the College of Integrated Philosophy in Edmonton, Canada, John was a humble Christian preacher and orthopedic shoemaker in rural Alberta. Now, his worldwide followers worship him as a new messiah.

The College of Integrated Philosophy holds regular "meetings" at the Oasis Centre, a seven million dollar facility that is hidden within an office park near the West Edmonton Mall and manned by an army of enthusiastic volunteers. Prior to acquiring the Oasis Centre, meetings were held in a small bookstore off of Whyte Avenue. His followers, mostly middle-aged women, are said to be completely "John Gone."

When I first heard about John, I was immediately intrigued. Was this movement simply new spiritual clothes for the emperor? Or was there something more to this staring guru and its cult of devotees? I had traveled to Edmonton to find out.

Forty-five minutes prior to the commencement of John's three-hour staring meeting, which cost ten dollars per head to attend and consisted of "dialogue and silent connection," the Oasis Centre was already packed to capacity. Before settling in, I decided to have lunch inside the facility at John's Jewel Café.

"I moved [to Edmonton] because of John," proclaimed a middle-aged woman standing next to me in the food line. It was already the umpteenth time that I had heard someone utter this phrase. The woman added, "Before I met John, I was living on a beach near Byron Bay (in Australia) and didn't even know where Edmonton was." So, she moved to Canada in search of something that she felt only John and his gaze could offer.

"Have you ever taken acid?" she inquired. "That's what it's like when you hear John. You listen and then suddenly something snaps and you get it."

That day, I hoped that I, too, would have an acid-snapping, spiritual staring moment. But if it didn't happen during the first meeting, according the gray-haired woman standing next to me as I grabbed a sandwich wrap, there were plenty more from which to choose: "Friday night we have a meeting. Sunday we have two meetings. Then, Monday we have another one," While smiling broadly, she added, "I go to all of them. I work here. So, Monday I go to work and just continue to stay here for the meeting, as well as Fridays."

John's world staring tour, which commenced shortly after my visit to Edmonton, included seminars in Israel, Germany, India, Holland, and England. And while tickets to meetings were a measly ten bucks, seminar tickets went for hundreds of dollars. Despite this hefty price tag, many of his devotees seemed willing to follow him around the globe.

"John goes to all these place. I go sometimes," said a kindly woman from New York. She had been a John follower for fifteen years before she decided to make the move to Edmonton. "I've been to Israel four times with John."

We sat down at a table with some women from Germany, Austria, Israel, and the United Kingdom. All of them stared intensely at me.

"It's very international," she continued. "You'll find that there are less Edmontonians than people from elsewhere, but they live in Edmonton now because of John."

The Israeli woman, who also moved to Canada because of John, asked me if I intended to sign-up to talk to him. "You put your name down if you want to talk to John," she instructed, "and you wait and see if your name comes up on the board."

I replied, "Maybe I shouldn't dive right into the deep end."

An older woman, who because of John moved from Austria to Edmonton five years earlier, offered advice: "It might seem really confusing at first at what's going on. No two meetings are the same. It all depends on who asks the questions. So, listen with your heart."

When she first attended one of John's seminars in Europe, she didn't speak a word of English, yet she claimed that she could understand everything he said. "I just knew he was speaking very important truths." She told me that no matter where John moved, she would follow him.

Before visiting the College of Integrated Philosophy, I spoke with University of Alberta in Edmonton Professor Stephen Kent, a cult expert who has researched de Ruiter's activities for years. "It's a community of striving, if not naive, followers," he said, describing the majority of members as Aquarian-aged people who grew up expecting the world to be filled with peace and happiness but have been left disappointed.

"John de Ruiter is maybe seen as the last hope of their generation to provide the kind of world they wanted," he told me. "People who want the world to be a good place and think it's attributing to its betterment but in fact are spending hours and hours of time listening to not a whole lot of insight."

Professor Kent stated that John's following has arisen as a result of the psychological process known as "misattribution," which is based on the notion that humans are meaning-seeking creatures. Followers, he said, misattribute John's relative silence and scarcity of words as indications of profound philosophical and spiritual depth.

"They expect a guru up there pontificating, but he doesn't say much. If you look at the message, there's not a lot of substance to it," he explained. "Many of the people are widely read in spirituality issues. They fill in the absence of the thoughts with their own knowledge and hopes and aspirations. So, they give John meaning that he himself may not even realize."

In the past, some members have expressed disillusionment with John's group, but few have come forward publicly to discuss their experiences. "They look around and perceive to see a large, happy community and then say, 'Oh, the problem must be with me. Everybody else sees the wisdom. So, it's my problem.' Then they feel that it's their shortcomings," said Professor Kent. "I'd say a lot of people have caught on, but they haven't spoken publicly about what they've come to realize."

According to Professor Kent, one woman left the group after she saw John at a gas station filling up his off-road truck. She asked the attendant if he knew John, and he told her that John came in all the time to have his truck repaired after off-road weekend trips. At that point, the woman realized that part of the money she was giving the group had been funding John's off-road hobby.

"Over a period of time, people have spent countless hours—and a fair amount of money—seeking out a product that is nonexistent. And when people finally realize what they've been doing for so long, it hits a lot of them really hard," added Professor Kent. "People are assigning wisdom to John based on what they have picked up themselves over the years. That sense of wisdom gets reinforced with members."

Professor Kent also has been told stories of arranged marriages that enabled foreign members to move to Edmonton, where they then became Oasis Centre volunteers. "I've heard that John will point at two people and say they should be married," he said. As a result, Professor Kent receives frequent calls from concerned family members and friends. "The devotion to John takes over people's lives. It inhibits the ability to make rational decisions for themselves and for their loved ones."

John's most public controversy involved two sisters, Benita and Katrina von Sass, with whom he was having an extramarital relationship. Not only did the sisters' father, businessman Peter von Sass, provide John with financial support, but he was the one who introduced John to his young, nubile daughters. (The story made the headlines in Canada since Katrina was a former Olympic volleyball player.)

At first, the staring guru denied the affair, stating that he was not answering questions on a "personal level." Later, he admitted to his congregation that "Truth" had told him to sleep with the von Sass sisters. John's wife refused to join the sister harem and divorced him. Eventually, the von Sass girls sued John, alleging that they were owed certain entitlements and payments from a decade spent as his common-law wives.

In an affidavit, Benita von Sass described John as "an opportunist and a huckster" who claimed to be "Christ on Earth." She alleged that he demanded her to "sexually submit to him" since it was "God's will." In addition to having regular sex with the two sisters, she claimed, John was still sleeping with his wife.

"There have been constant rumors about affairs, and members either don't take them seriously or don't care," said Professor Kent. "They believe he is operating on a different level of wisdom that puts him in a different realm from the rest of us and gives him permissions that normal people don't have."

It was time for the main event. I wanted to understand how John could wield so much power with a mere look.

"What John emphasizes is that it's not about anything he is

saying. It's really about opening your heart and seeing what you see and what opens for you," said a volunteer from Holland who, after attending John's summer seminar, moved to Edmonton and became engaged to another member. "Sometimes it could be far out there, based on so much knowledge and foundation and common understanding," she said, acknowledging that at some of the three-hour meetings John doesn't speak at all.

So, I was going to try—as instructed—to keep my heart and mind open.

I paid for my ten dollar ticket and drew an assigned seat. Up front and close to the stage was the gold circle, where attendees got the most impact of John's direct stare.

"I'm in the boonies," lamented a woman who had been coming to meetings since 1996.

Her friend replied, "You've been here for so long, you don't need any more close-ups." They laughed.

The Oasis Centre's lavish auditorium was designed solely for John and his staring proclivities. Adorned with ornate chandeliers, a proscenium stage, and marble pillars, the venue was worthy of a king—or a spiritual guru with followers who moved from all corners of the world to be closer to his gaze. I learned that the College of Integrated Philosophy sometimes rents out the luxurious facility for wedding receptions, which during peak season can cost up to thirteen thousand dollars.

As I took my seat off to the side, roughly three-hundred fifty people filtered into the auditorium, almost filling it to capacity.

"I've been to about four thousand meetings," said the young woman sitting next to me. "I started coming when I was seven [years old]." Originally from Vancouver, the woman moved to Edmonton with her parents when she was a child "because of John."

Once everyone was seated, a British woman came onstage to tell the crowd about the scholarship fund for those who could not afford John's seminars. "Those requesting a scholarship may be asked to look at their lifestyle and find new ways to contribute to these seminars financially," she said, attempting to provide a brief training workshop for budgeting. "This could include simple suggestions like setting up a toonie jar (a piggy bank), comprehensive budget planning, managing resources, considering downsizing, or renting a room or a garage out."

I tried to keep my heart open as John's devotees provided instructions, despite the fact that this woman had just encouraged his followers to rent out rooms in their homes to help pay for John's expensive seminars.

Suddenly, the energy dramatically shifted, and an eerie stillness fell upon the room. Music no longer emanated throughout the auditorium. It was just silence (and a few coughs). We were acutely aware of John's presence as he stood on the side of the stage for what seemed like an incredibly long amount of time. Finally, John slowly walked towards his large comfy chair; his footsteps loudly reverberated throughout the hushed auditorium, creating a mausoleum-esque atmosphere. John sat down and, with dramatic effect, slowly put on his headset.

With his face projected onto the large video screens, John began staring—in what was probably the world's largest staring contest. His eyes glistened like pooled Visine. It was hard not to break into a smug Richard Dawkins laugh, but this meeting was a no-nonsense affair. So, I clamped down on my giggling.

Occasionally, the video monitors cut to shots of the crowd staring at John. It was almost like being in church—a church where the pastor had just had a stroke and all he could do was stare at you. This nonsense continued for about an hour until John went one by one and stared directly at each person in attendance. When he looked at me, my heart fluttered, and I realized how uncomfortable it was to be stared at by non-blinking eyes.

In order to feel what his followers must have felt, I tried melting into his stare, his handsome face, his pouty lips, and his steely blue eyes. Staring at John was like staring at a glassy-eyed Dutch painting. After a while, it started to feel as if he was staring solely at me, which, as a result of the utter silence, felt incredibly intimate. The auditorium was packed, but it felt as if it were just John and me.

Then, abruptly, the spell was broken. John's large, staring head on the video screen started to remind me of the psychics in David Cronenberg's *Scanners*, and I was afraid his head might explode. Maybe I was beginning to read too much into this grift. Doubtful, because things were about to turn weird (well, even weirder than before).

After taking a seat in the chair directly in front of John, a teary-eyed woman, who had signed-up to ask questions of him, appeared on the video screens. She was a fragile mess and spoke rather slowly as John stared at her. "It's important for me to speak to you. I have a really hard time articulating," she said. "I don't have a question; I just love what I'm responding to. I just so love responding. It's not even a choice; it's just happening. I have no direct experience what is now, but I love our bond." The two adults continued to stare at each other, which was eventually followed by a long pause and strained coughs. "I don't know what this is, but somehow we are in this together in some sweet way."

As John and the woman stared at each other, we stared at them. I wondered who would blink first.

Professor Kent told me that in the early days of John's meetings anyone could ask John a question. That day there was a preliminary screening process; if they didn't like what a person was prepared to say, then they weren't called upon.

"How to see the speck of gold that has no weight—it is weightless?" asked a Dutch woman who was now in John's hot seat.

After a long pause, John, at last, spoke: "You enjoy knowing the gold directly." His words were slow, soft, and deliberate.

The crowd had been waiting for hours for John to speak, and finally, he was speaking. So, I assumed his words must have been extremely important. He continued: "It is real to you, the gold. You respond to what you know is golden. You see that which is most deeply real in you."

With a slow and torturous cadence, John threw out more fortune cookie Haiku statements, such as this gem: "The plow breaks the ground in yourself. When you are in flow, do what is golden. That which is not golden breaks."

John's followers stared intently, hanging onto every word and creating meaning out of nothingness. The Dutch woman continued questioning John with an equally slow delivery. It was as if I were watching two people high on mescaline trying to hold a conversation.

"I feel small," she said.

After some time, John replied, "You feel that because your self is too small for you."

The woman's chest heaved with each question as John continued his dreamy, hypnotic dialogue, when it suited him. Sometimes she said things, and John didn't respond. Instead, he just kept staring uncomfortably at her.

Finally, John pulled out what I assumed to be his most popular parlor trick: he shed a solitary tear that slowly trickled down his cheek. The entire auditorium gasped in unison.

"Tell me to stop, because I could go on forever," said the Dutch woman. John remained silent. The two stared down each other for another ten minutes, until John abruptly removed his headset and walked off the stage.

I felt confused. Had I missed something? John seemed to provide people with a sense of happiness, but all I saw was underlying confusion and sadness.

"It's a lot to take in for the first time," I said to the kindly New York woman as we exited the auditorium for our dinner break in John's Jewel Café.

"John opens the door for you and gives you the direction," she explained. "Once the door is open, you're there." I asked her to elaborate. "It's not a practice like Buddhism," she replied. "It's more direct. This is direct knowledge, a direct transmission, and John's a portal to it. He awakens the answers within you."

I responded, "Sometimes you can say a lot more without words."

A man from London overheard our conversation and offered his own interpretation of the profound depth: "Life is uneventful; it's meant to be uneventful."

Trying to connect the spiritual dots, I asked the Austrian woman, "Is that how it usually is, where he channels the answers within the person?"

Attempting to clarify, she responded, "It's not channeling; it's so much more. It's what the person can see. You came to a very special meeting. You're lucky!"

Since I had made the trek all the way to Edmonton, I decided that I might as well stay for the second session, which meant I was moving into my fifth hour of staring. Although it started similarly, this one, maybe, was not as special as the first as yet another attractive and teary-eyed woman stepped into John's hot seat. Her question had to do with hysterically sobbing on the drive home from a meeting.

"Your deeper womanist is more than yourself," John said slowly before staring at her for a long period of time and finally adding: "It has no past. It flows without a path."

With obvious frustration, she asked, "Can you say more about that? I really want to know more."

John replied, "Use the pathways into yourself. But it still has no path as your deeper womanist moves through the pathways of yourself. As it moves through yourself, it will change yourself, your deeper womanist."

Wanting more, the woman inquired, "Is my deeper womanist an aspect of my being?"

John sat unmoved. He did not blink. Was he channeling the answer? Or did he not have an answer? After several minutes of silence and staring, John said, "Without a self, it has no purpose."

The woman seemed frustrated by the painfully long silence between each response. "I am not affected by how you are not responding," she confessed.

John gave the woman his silent, steely stare. Was John helping this emotionally fragile woman who was willing to believe everything he said—no matter how slowly he said it—with blind devotion? Or was he a charlatan conducting an elaborate parlor trick for the vulnerable and weak?

The man sitting next to me looked as if he had been dragged to the "meeting" by his wife. He started to doze off—boredom followed by silence followed by nothingness ...

# AFTERWORD

IN OUR PERSONAL QUESTS to find acceptance from our peers, we often find ourselves, wittingly or unwittingly, as a member of a tribe of (what we think are) like-minded people. Whether it's joining others in brandishing an AK-47, putting on a hand-crafted furry suit, digging through trash bins for gourmet food, adoring that certain celebrity, or staring at a silent but handsome man, the desire to find a sense of community with our fellow enthusiasts is a normal part of the human experience. There is nothing inherently wrong in seeking out—and joining with—others who share similar interests and appear to embody our ideals and values.

But for some individuals, it's easy to become intoxicated by the mob mentality of a group. The seductive powers of tribalism can be pervasive, controlling our behaviors and overriding our better reason. According to Scottish philosopher David Hume, the "human mind is of a very imitative nature," and it is not possible for people to converse together "without acquiring a similitude of manners."

As part of a tribe that has acquired a "similitude of manners," we don't have to think independently about (or objectively analyze) the issues at hand. By blindly following the edicts of our charismatic tribal leaders, we know exactly what side we are on and what to believe, despite the terrible things that are sometimes said and done in the name of tribal unity.

Suspicions, however, should arise when our individual principles and morals become compromised by the whims of the tribal leader, who—in an effort to control and exploit the tribe—breaks down discourse to its lowest common denominator: us versus them. The misuse of tribal loyalty by tribal leaders to demonize others is a breech of trust and results in toxic conduct, causing some people to become so consumed with their tribal identities that they are incapable of comprehending points of view inconsistent with their own. They ignore basic facts and regard those with different beliefs as the enemy, whose lives are foreign, incomprehensible, and repulsive.

When the commitment of disciples to a tribe becomes so intense that no matter what the tribal leader says or does—no matter how despicable, horrible, or offensive—that we haphazardly follow with cult-like fervor, we have departed from reality and lost our way. All of society suffers.

Not until we question our own assumptions, open our minds to new perspectives, and learn to treat our fellow humans with kindness, compassion, and empathy can we overcome tribal divisiveness and put an end to the suffering and destruction currently plaguing our nation. It all starts with you.

# ACKNOWLEDGMENTS

Harmon Leon is grateful to the editors of the following books and periodicals where his work first appeared:

### BOOKS

*The Infiltrator: My Undercover Exploits in Right-Wing America* (Prometheus Books, 2006): "Machine Gun Shooters"

*Republican Like Me: Infiltrating Red-State, White-Ass, and Blue-Suit America* (Prometheus Books, 2005): "Body-slammin' for Jesus," "White Supremacists"

### PERIODICALS

*Penthouse*: "Furries," "Hookers for Jesus," "Jump for Jesus," "Staring Cult"

*Playboy's The Smoking Jacket*: "Pickup Artists"

*SFGate*: "Trophy Wife Hunters"

*Vice*: "Christian Comics," "Cuban Comics," "Drunk Santas," "Fans of 'The Juice,'" "Fans of Jerry Springer" "Freegans," "Presidential Joke Writers," "Squatters," "Tanning Addicts," "Viral Video Fans"

*The Wave*: "The Raëlians"

# IMAGE CREDITS

All **(th)ink** and **The K Chronicles** cartoons by Keith Knight.

**KEITH KNIGHT** is many things to many people—rapper, social activist, father, and educator among them. He's also one of the funniest and most highly regarded cartoonists in America and the creator of three popular comic strips: *The Knight Life*, *(th)ink*, and *The K Chronicles*. For nearly two decades, Knight, a multi-award-winning artist, has brought the funny back to the funny pages with a uniquely personal style that's a cross between *Calvin & Hobbes*, *MAD*, and underground comix. Knight is part of a generation of African-American artists who were raised on hip-hop and infuse their work with urgency, edge, humor, satire, politics, and race. His art has appeared in various publications worldwide, including the *Washington Post*, *Daily KOS*, *San Francisco Chronicle*, *Medium.com*, *Ebony*, *ESPN the Magazine*, *L.A. Weekly*, *MAD*, and *Funny Times*. Find his work online at www.kchronicles.com.

## ABOUT THE AUTHOR

**HARMON LEON** is a journalist, comedian, and filmmaker. He is the author of seven previous books, including *Meet the Deplorables: Infiltrating Trump America*, as well as *The Harmon Chronicles* and *Republican Like Me*, which both won Independent Publisher Awards for humor. Leon's writing can be found in *Vice*, *The Nation*, *The Observer*, *Esquire*, *Ozy*, *National Geographic*, *The Guardian*, *Wired*, and more. He has appeared on *This American Life*, *The Howard Stern Show*, *Penn and Teller: Bullshit!*, *Last Call with Carson Daly*, MSNBC, and the BBC and has performed his critically-acclaimed solo comedy shows at venues around the world, including The Edinburgh Festival, Melbourne Comedy Festival, and Montreal's Just for Laughs. Leon is the producer of a recent Official Selection at the Sundance Film Festival and the host of a popular podcast: *Comedy History 101*. Visit him online at www.harmonleon.com.

www.ingramcontent.com/pod-product-compliance
Lightning Source LLC
Chambersburg PA
CBHW030111100526
44591CB00009B/365